Congressional Research Service

Informing the legislative debate since 1914

Border Security: Immigration Enforcement Between Ports of Entry

Lisa Seghetti
Section Research Manager

January 16, 2014

Congressional Research Service

7-5700

www.crs.gov

R42138

Summary

Border enforcement is a core element of the Department of Homeland Security's (DHS's) effort to control unauthorized migration, with the U.S. Border Patrol (USBP) within the Bureau of Customs and Border Protection (CBP) as the lead agency along most of the border. Border enforcement has been an ongoing subject of congressional interest since the 1970s, when illegal immigration to the United States first registered as a serious national problem; and border security has received additional attention in the years since the terrorist attacks of 2001.

Since the 1990s, migration control at the border has been guided by a strategy of "prevention through deterrence"—the idea that the concentration of personnel, infrastructure, and surveillance technology along heavily trafficked regions of the border will discourage unauthorized aliens from attempting to enter the United States. Since 2005, CBP has attempted to discourage repeat entries and disrupt migrant smuggling networks by imposing tougher penalties against certain unauthorized aliens, a set of policies eventually described as "enforcement with consequences." Most people apprehended at the Southwest border are now subject to "high consequence" enforcement outcomes.

Across a variety of indicators, the United States has substantially expanded border enforcement resources over the last three decades. Particularly since 2001, such increases include border security appropriations, personnel, fencing and infrastructure, and surveillance technology.

The Border Patrol collects data on several different border enforcement outcomes; and this report describes trends in border apprehensions, recidivism, and estimated got aways and turn backs. Yet none of these existing data are designed to measure illegal border flows or the degree to which the border is secured. Thus, the report also describes methods for estimating illegal border flows based on enforcement data and migrant surveys.

Drawing on multiple data sources, the report suggests conclusions about the state of border security. Robust investments at the border were not associated with reduced illegal inflows during the 1980s and 1990s, but a range of evidence suggests a substantial drop in illegal inflows in 2007-2011, followed by a slight rise in 2012. Enforcement, along with the economic downturn in the United States, likely contributed to the drop in unauthorized migration, though the precise share of the decline attributable to enforcement is unknown.

Enhanced border enforcement also may have contributed to a number of secondary costs and benefits. To the extent that border enforcement successfully deters illegal entries, such enforcement may reduce border-area violence and migrant deaths, protect fragile border ecosystems, and improve the quality of life in border communities. But to the extent that aliens are not deterred, the concentration of enforcement resources on the border may increase border area violence and migrant deaths, encourage unauthorized migrants to find new ways to enter illegally and to remain in the United States for longer periods of time, damage border ecosystems, harm border-area businesses and the quality of life in border communities, and strain U.S. relations with Mexico and Canada.

Contents

Figures

Tables

Appendixes

Contacts

Introduction

The country's immigration and naturalization laws have been subjects of episodic controversy since America's founding, but *illegal* immigration only became an issue in the early 20th century, when Congress passed the first strict restrictions on legal admissions. Illegal immigration declined during the Great Depression and during and after World War II, when most labor migration occurred through the U.S.-Mexico Bracero program.[1] Immigration control re-emerged as a national concern during the 1970s, when the end of the Bracero program, new restrictions on Western Hemisphere migration, and growing U.S. demand for foreign-born workers combined to cause a sharp increase in unauthorized migration flows.[2]

Congress responded in 1986 by passing the Immigration Reform and Control Act (IRCA, P.L. 99-603), which authorized a 50% increase in Border Patrol staffing, among other provisions. Border security[3] has remained a persistent topic of congressional interest since then, and enforcement programs and appropriations have grown accordingly, as described in this report.

Despite a growing enforcement response, however, illegal immigration continued to increase over most of the next three decades, with the estimated unauthorized population peaking at 12.4 million people in 2007.[4] Unauthorized migration has declined since 2007, with the estimated unauthorized population falling to 11.5 million in 2011.[5] Apprehensions of unauthorized migrants at the U.S.-Mexico border fell from about 1.2 million in 2005 to a 41-year low of 328,000 in 2011, before climbing slightly to 357,000 in 2012.[6]

The Obama Administration cites falling apprehensions, among other statistics, as evidence that the border is more secure than ever.[7] Yet some Members of Congress and others disagree and have called on the Administration to do more to secure the border. Border security has been a recurrent theme in Congress's debate about comprehensive immigration reform since 2005, and some Members of Congress have argued that Congress should not consider additional immigration reforms until the border is more secure.[8]

---

[1] The Bracero program was a formal guest worker program managed jointly by the United States and Mexico that admitted about 4.6 million workers between 1942 and 1964.

[2] The estimated population of unauthorized aliens was about 1.7 million by 1979 and about 3.2 million in 1986; most researchers, however, consider earlier estimates of the unauthorized population to be unreliable. See Jennifer Van Hook and Frank D. Bean, "Estimating Unauthorized Mexican Migration to the United States: Issues and Trends," in *Binational Study: Migration Between Mexico and the United States* (Washington, DC: US Commission on Immigration Reform, 1998), pp. 538-540.

[3] Except as otherwise noted, this report focuses exclusively on border security as it relates to the prevention of unauthorized migration. On the relationship among unauthorized migration, illegal drugs and other contraband, international terrorists, and other types of border threats, see CRS Report R42969, *Border Security: Understanding Threats at U.S. Borders*, by Jerome P. Bjelopera and Kristin Finklea.

[4] CRS Report RL33874, *Unauthorized Aliens Residing in the United States: Estimates Since 1986*, by Ruth Ellen Wasem.

[5] Ibid.

[6] United States Border Patrol (USBP), "Southwest Border Sectors: Total Apprehensions by Fiscal Year," http://www.cbp.gov/linkhandler/cgov/border_security/border_patrol/usbp_statistics/usbp_fy12_stats/nationwide_appr_2000_2012.ctt/nationwide_appr_2000_2012.pdf.

[7] See for example, the White House, "Fixing the Immigration System for America's 21st Century Economy," http://www.whitehouse.gov/issues/fixing-immigration-system-america-s-21st-century-economy.

[8] See, for example, Alan Gomez, "Border Security Quandary Could Kill Immigration Bill," *USA Today*, April 2, 2013.

This report reviews efforts to combat unauthorized migration across the Southwest border in the nearly three decades since IRCA initiated the modern era in migration control. In reviewing such efforts, the report takes stock of the current state of border security and considers lessons that may be learned about enhanced enforcement at U.S. borders. The report begins by reviewing the history of border control and the development of a national border control strategy beginning in the 1990s. The following sections summarize appropriations and resources dedicated to border enforcement, indicators of enforcement outcomes, metrics for estimating unauthorized migration flows, and possible secondary and unintended consequences of border enforcement. The report concludes by reviewing the overall costs and benefits of the current approach to migration control and raising additional questions that may help guide the discussion of these issues in the future.

Border Patrol History and Strategy

Congress created the U.S. Border Patrol (USBP) within the Department of Commerce and Labor by an appropriations act in 1924,[9] two days after passing the first permanent numeric immigration restrictions.[10] Numerical limits only applied to the Eastern Hemisphere, barring most Asian immigration; and the Border Patrol's initial focus was on preventing the entry of Chinese migrants, as well as combating gun trafficking and alcohol imports during prohibition. The majority of agents were stationed on the northern border.[11] The Border Patrol became part of the new Immigration and Naturalization Service (INS) in 1933, and the INS moved from the Department of Labor to the Department of Justice in 1940. The Border Patrol's focus shifted to the Southwest border during World War II, but preventing illegal migration across the Southwest border remained a low priority during most of the 20th century.[12]

Illegal migration from Mexico increased after 1965 as legislative changes restricted legal Mexican immigration at the same time that social and economic changes caused stronger migration "pushes" in Mexico (e.g., inadequate employment opportunities) and stronger "pulls" in the United States (e.g., employment opportunities, links to migrant communities in Mexico).[13] Congress held hearings on illegal immigration beginning in 1971, and after more than a decade of debate passed the Immigration Reform and Control Act of 1986 (IRCA, P.L. 99-603), which described border enforcement as an "essential element" of immigration control and authorized a 50% increase in funding for the Border Patrol, among other provisions.[14] Congress passed at least

---

[9] Act of May 28, 1924; (43 Stat. 240).

[10] Immigration Act of May 26, 1924 (43 Stat. 153).

[11] See U.S. Customs and Border Protection (CBP), "Border Patrol History," http://www.cbp.gov/xp/cgov/border_security/border_patrol/border_patrol_ohs/history xml.

[12] See Kitty Calavita, *Inside the State: The Bracero Program, Immigration, and the I.N.S.* (New York: Routledge, 1992); Mark Reisler, *By the Sweat of Their Brow: Mexican Immigrant Labor in the United States, 1900-1940* (Westport, CT: Greenwood Press, 1976); Douglas S. Massey, Jorge Durand, and Nolan J. Malone, *Beyond Smoke and Mirrors: Mexican Immigration in an Era of Economic Integration* (New York: Russell Sage Foundation, 2002).

[13] See CRS Report R42560, *Mexican Migration to the United States: Policy and Trends*, by William A. Kandel, Clare Ribando Seelke, and Ruth Ellen Wasem. Legislative changes included the termination of the U.S.-Mexican Bracero guest worker program in 1965 and the imposition of numeric limits on migration from Mexico and other Western Hemisphere countries pursuant to the Immigration and Nationality Act Amendments of 1965 (P.L. 89-236).

[14] See U.S. Congress, House Committee on the Judiciary, The "Immigration Reform and Control Act of 1986" (P.L. 99-603), 99th Cong., 2nd Sess., December 1986, H. Rept. 99-14 (Washington: GPO, 1986).

11 additional laws addressing illegal immigration over the next two decades, 7 of which included provisions related to the border.[15]

Border Patrol Strategic Plans

Seventy years after it began operations, the Border Patrol developed its first formal national border control strategy in 1994, the National Strategic Plan. The plan was updated in 2004 and again in 2012.

National Strategic Plan

The National Strategic Plan (NSP) was developed in 1994 in response to a widespread perception that the Southwest border was being overrun by unauthorized immigration and drug smuggling, and to respond to a study commissioned by the Office of National Drug Control Policy. The study recommended that the INS change its approach from arresting unauthorized immigrants after they enter the United States, as had previously been the case, to focus instead on preventing their entry.[16] Under the new approach, the INS would place personnel, surveillance technology, fencing, and other infrastructure directly on the border to discourage illegal flows, a strategy that became known as "prevention through deterrence." According to the 1994 INS plan, "the prediction is that with traditional entry and smuggling routes disrupted, illegal traffic will be deterred, or forced over more hostile terrain, less suited for crossing and more suited for enforcement."[17]

The strategy had four phases that began with the border patrol sectors with the highest levels of illegal immigration activity.

- Phase I: San Diego, CA, and El Paso, TX, sectors;

- Phase II: Tucson, AZ, Del Rio, TX, Laredo, TX, and McAllen, TX, sectors;

- Phase III: El Centro, CA, Yuma, AZ, and Marfa, TX, sectors; and

- Phase IV: The northern border, gulf coast, and coastal waterways

The strategy yielded several initiatives aimed at stemming illegal immigration and human smuggling, and interdicting drug trafficking. These initiatives included the following:

- *Operation Gatekeeper* was first initiated at the San Diego Border Patrol Sector and was later extended to the El Centro Border Patrol Sector. The initiative

---

[15] The seven laws that included border-related provisions were the Immigration Act of 1990 (P.L. 101-649), the Illegal Immigration Reform and Immigrant Responsibility Act of 1996 (P.L. 104-208, Div. C), the USA-PATRIOT Act of 2002 (P.L. 107-56), the Homeland Security Act of 2002 (P.L. 107-296), the Intelligence Reform and Terrorism Prevention Act of 2004 (108-458), the REAL-ID Act of 2005 (P.L. 109-13, Div. B), and the Secure Fence Act of 2006 (P.L. 109-367).

[16] U.S. Office of National Drug Control Policy, *National Drug Control Strategy: Reclaiming Our Communities from Drugs and Violence* (Washington, DC: U.S. Department of Justice, 1994), https://www.ncjrs.gov/pdffiles1/ondcp/150489.pdf.

[17] U.S. Border Patrol, *Border Patrol Strategic Plan: 1994 and Beyond*, July 1994, pp. 6-7 (Hereinafter, National Strategic Plan).

involved providing border patrol agents with additional resources, such as increased staffing and new technologies.

- *Operation Safeguard* was initiated at the Tucson Border Patrol Sector and was aimed at stemming illegal immigration by pushing illegal immigrants away from urban areas.

- *Operation Hold the Line* was initiated at the El Paso Border Patrol Sector and was aimed at the specific needs of the community. New border patrol agents were added to the area and innovative resources were deployed, including IDENT[18] terminals. The initiative also included the installation of fences along parts of the border and other infrastructure improvements.

- Operation Rio Grande was initiated at the McAllen Border Patrol Sector and focused on increasing the number of border patrol agents.

The implementation of Phase II and subsequent phases was to be based on the success of Phase I, with the plan describing several expected indicators of effective border enforcement, including an initial increase of border arrests and entry attempt to be followed by an eventual reduction of arrests, a change in traditional traffic patterns, and an increase in more sophisticated smuggling methods.[19] As predicted, apprehensions within the San Diego and El Paso sectors fell sharply beginning in 1994-1995, and traffic patterns shifted, primarily to the Tucson and South Texas (Rio Grande Valley) sectors (see "Southwest Border Apprehensions by Sector"). A 1997 General Accounting Office (GAO) report was cautiously optimistic about the strategy.[20]

Congress supported the prevention through deterrence approach. In 1996, House and Senate appropriators directed the INS to hire new agents and to reallocate personnel from the interior to front line duty.[21] And the Illegal Immigration Reform and Immigrant Responsibility Act of 1996 (P.L. 104-208) expressly authorized the construction and improvement of fencing and other barriers along the Southwest border and required the completion of a triple-layered fence along 14 miles of the border near San Diego where the INS had begun to install fencing in 1990.[22]

National Border Patrol Strategy

In the wake of the September 11, 2001, terrorist attacks, the USBP refocused its priorities on preventing terrorist penetration, while remaining committed to its traditional duties of preventing the illicit trafficking of people and contraband between official ports of entry. Shortly after the creation of DHS, the USBP was directed to formulate a new National Border Patrol Strategy

---

[18] The Automated Biometric Identification (IDENT) system is DHS's primary biometric database. Certain aliens' biometric records are added to IDENT upon admission to the United States, when aliens are apprehended or arrested by a DHS agency, and when aliens apply for certain immigration benefits.

[19] National Strategic Plan, pp. 9-10.

[20] U.S. General Accounting Office, *Illegal Immigration: Southwest Border Strategy Results Inconclusive; More Evaluation Needed*, GAO/GGD-98-21, December 1997.

[21] U.S. Congress, Senate Committee on Appropriations, *Departments of Commerce, Justice, and State, The Judiciary, and Related Agencies Appropriations Bill, 1996*, report to accompany H.R. 2076, 104th Cong., 1st sess., S.Rept. 104-139 and U.S. Congress, House Committee on Appropriations, *Making Appropriations for the Departments of Commerce, Justice, and State, The Judiciary, and Related Agencies For the Fiscal Year Ending September 30, 1996, and for Other Purposes*, report to accompany H.R. 2076, 104th Cong., 1st sess., H.Rept. 104-378.

[22] P.L. 104-208, Div. C §102.

(NBPS) that would better reflect the realities of the post-9/11 security landscape. In March 2004, the Border Patrol unveiled the National Border Patrol Strategy, which placed greater emphasis on interdicting terrorists and featured five main objectives:

- establishing the substantial probability of apprehending terrorists and their weapons as they attempt to enter illegally between the ports of entry;

- deterring illegal entries through improved enforcement;

- detecting, apprehending, and deterring smugglers of humans, drugs, and other contraband;

- leveraging "Smart Border" technology to multiply the deterrent and enforcement effect of agents; and

- reducing crime in border communities, thereby improving the quality of life and economic vitality of those areas.[23]

The NBPS was an attempt to lay the foundation for achieving "operational control" over the border, defined by the Border Patrol as "the ability to detect, respond, and interdict border penetrations in areas deemed as high priority for threat potential or other national security objectives."[24] The strategy emphasized a hierarchical and vertical command structure, featuring a direct chain of command from headquarters to the field. The document emphasized the use of tactical, operational, and strategic intelligence and sophisticated surveillance systems to assess risk and target enforcement efforts; and the rapid deployment of USBP agents to respond to emerging threats. Additionally, the plan called for the Border Patrol to coordinate closely with CBP's Office of Intelligence and other federal intelligence agencies.

Border Patrol Strategic Plan

CBP published a new Border Patrol Strategic Plan (BPSP) in May 2012 that shifted attention from resource acquisition and deployment to the strategic allocation of resources by "focusing enhanced capabilities against the highest threats and rapidly responding along the border."[25] From an operational perspective, the 2012 plan emphasizes the collection and analysis of information about evolving border threats; integration of Border Patrol and CBP planning across different border sectors and among the full range of federal, state, local, tribal, and international organizations involved in border security operations; and rapid Border Patrol response to specific border threats.[26]

DHS Secure Border Initiative

The Border Patrol's approach to border enforcement has been mirrored in broader DHS policies. In November 2005, the Department of Homeland Security announced a comprehensive multi-

---

[23] Department of Homeland Security, Bureau of Customs and Border Protection, *National Border Patrol Strategy*, March 1, 2005. Hereinafter, *USBP National Strategy*.

[24] *USBP National Strategy*, p. 3. This definition differs from the statutory definition found in Section 2 of the Secure Fence Act of 2006 (P.L. 109-367); see in this report "**Operational Control of the Border**."

[25] CBP, *2012-2016 Border Patrol Strategic Plan*, Washington, DC: 2012, p. 7.

[26] Ibid.

year plan, the Secure Border Initiative (SBI), to secure U.S. borders and reduce illegal migration.[27] Under SBI, DHS announced plans to obtain operational control of the northern and southern borders within five years by focusing attention in five main areas:

- **Increased staffing**. As part of SBI, DHS announced the addition of 1,000 new Border Patrol agents, 250 new ICE investigators targeting human smuggling operations, and 500 other new ICE agents and officers.[28]

- **Improved detention and removal capacity**. Historically, most non-Mexicans apprehended at the border were placed in formal removal proceedings.[29] Yet backlogs in the immigration court system meant that most such aliens were released on bail or on their own recognizance prior to a removal hearing, and many failed to show up for their hearings.[30] In October 2005, DHS announced plans to detain 100% of non-Mexicans apprehended at the border until they could be processed for removal. SBI supported this goal by adding detention capacity, initially increasing bed space by 2,000 to a total of 20,000.[31] On August 23, 2006, DHS announced that the policy to "end catch and release" had been successfully implemented.[32]

- **Surveillance technology**. SBI included plans to expand DHS's use of surveillance technology between ports of entry, including unmanned aerial vehicle (UAV) systems, other aerial assets, remote video surveillance (RVS) systems, and ground sensors.[33] These tools were to be linked into a common integrated system that became known as SBI*net* (see "Surveillance Assets" below).

- **Tactical infrastructure**. SBI continued DHS's commitment to the expansion of border fencing, roads, and stadium-style lighting.[34]

- **Interior enforcement**. SBI also included plans to expand enforcement within the United States at worksites and through state and local partnerships, jail screening programs, and task forces to locate fugitive aliens.[35]

---

[27] DHS, "Fact Sheet: Secure Border Initiative," https://www.hsdl.org/?view&did=440470.

[28] Ibid.

[29] Prior to 1996, the INA included distinct provisions for the "exclusion" of inadmissible aliens and the "deportation" of certain aliens from within the United States. Pursuant to §§301-309 of the Illegal Immigration Reform and Immigrant Responsibility Act of 1996 (IIRIRA, P.L. 104-208, Div. C), deportation and exclusion proceedings were combined into a unified "removal" proceeding (8 U.S.C. 1229a). This report uses "deportation" to refer to the compulsory return of aliens to their country of origin prior to the implementation of IIRIRA in 1997, and "removal" to refer to aliens returned under these provisions since 1997.

[30] DHS estimated that there were 623,292 alien "absconders" in August 2006, many of whom had failed to appear for removal hearings after being apprehended at the border; see Doris Meissner and Donald Kerwin, *DHS and Immigration: Taking Stock and Correcting Course*, Migration Policy Institute, Washington, DC, February 2009, p. 44, http://www.migrationpolicy.org/pubs/DHS_Feb09.pdf.

[31] DHS, "Fact Sheet: Secure Border Initiative," https://www.hsdl.org/?view&did=440470.

[32] CBP, "DHS Secretary Announces End to 'Catch and Release' on Southern Border," http://www.cbp.gov/xp/cgov/admin/c1_archive/messages/end_catch_release.xml.

[33] DHS, "Fact Sheet: Secure Border Initiative," https://www.hsdl.org/?view&did=440470.

[34] Ibid.

[35] Ibid. Interior enforcement programs are not discussed in this report; see CRS Report R42057, *Interior Immigration Enforcement: Programs Targeting Criminal Aliens*, by William A. Kandel; and CRS Report R40002, *Immigration-* (continued...)

CBP Consequence Delivery System

Although not the subject of a formal public policy document like those discussed above, an additional component of CBP's approach to border control in recent years has been an effort to promote "high consequence" enforcement for unauthorized Mexicans apprehended at the border.[36] Historically, immigration agents permitted most Mexicans apprehended at the border to voluntarily return to Mexico without any penalty.[37] Since 2005, CBP has limited voluntary returns in favor of three types of "high consequence" outcomes:

- **Formal Removal**.[38] Aliens[39] formally removed from the United States generally are ineligible for a visa (i.e., inadmissible) for at least five years,[40] and they may be subject to criminal charges if they illegally reenter the United States.[41] Prior to 2005, most unauthorized Mexicans apprehended at the border were not placed in removal proceedings, in part because standard removal procedures require an appearance before an immigration judge and are resource intensive. Since 2005, CBP has relied extensively on two provisions in the Immigration and Nationality Act (INA) that permit aliens to be formally removed with limited judicial processing. Under INA Section 235(b), certain arriving aliens are subject to "expedited removal" (ER) without additional hearing or review.[42] ER was added to the INA in 1996, but initially was reserved for aliens apprehended at ports of entry. In a series of four announcements between November 2002 and January 2006, DHS expanded the use of ER to include certain aliens who had entered the United States within the previous two weeks and who were apprehended anywhere within 100 miles of a U.S. land or coastal border.[43] Under INA Section 241(a)(5), an alien who reenters the United States after being formally removed or departing under a removal order is subject to "reinstatement of removal" without reopening or reviewing the original removal order.[44]

(...continued)

Related Worksite Enforcement: Performance Measures, by Andorra Bruno.

[36] Prior to development of the Consequence Delivery System, most non-Mexican aliens already were placed in formal removal proceedings and, after 2005, were normally detained until a removal order was implemented (see in this report **"DHS Secure Border Initiative"**).

[37] Section 240B of the INA permits immigration agents and judges to allow certain removable aliens to "voluntarily depart" the United States. In contrast with aliens subject to formal removal, aliens subject to voluntary departure generally do not face additional immigration-related penalties.

[38] Pursuant to §§301-309 of the Illegal Immigration Reform and Immigrant Responsibility Act of 1996 (IIRIRA, P.L. 104-208, Div. C), deportation and exclusion proceedings were combined into a unified "removal" proceeding (INA §240); and immigration judges were given discretion to permit aliens who are subject to removal to "voluntarily depart" in lieu of facing formal removal proceedings (INA §240B).

[39] "Aliens" is synonymous with non-citizens, including legal permanent residents, temporary nonimmigrants, and unauthorized aliens.

[40] INA §212(a)(9).

[41] INA §276.

[42] Aliens who indicate an intention to apply for asylum or a fear of persecution are not subject to formal removal; for a fuller discussion of expedited removal see CRS Report RL33109, *Immigration Policy on Expedited Removal of Aliens*, by Alison Siskin and Ruth Ellen Wasem.

[43] Ibid. Under the 2006 policy, most Mexicans apprehended at the Southwest border were not placed in expedited removal proceedings unless they had previous criminal convictions.

[44] CBP's expanded use of reinstatement of removal depended, in part, on its ability to identify repeat offenders by enrolling their biometric data in the Automated Biometric Identification System (IDENT) system, a database of over (continued...)

- **Criminal Charges**. Unauthorized aliens apprehended at the border may face federal immigration charges,[45] but historically, most such aliens have not been charged with a crime. Working with the Department of Justice (DOJ), DHS has increased the proportion of people apprehended at the border who are charged with immigration-related criminal offenses. About half of aliens facing criminal charges in Southwest border districts are prosecuted through the "Operation Streamline" program (see accompanying text box). Mexicans apprehended in the United States who are found to be smuggling aliens may also be subject to criminal charges in Mexico under the U.S.-Mexican Operation Against Smugglers Initiative on Safety and Security (OASISS).[46]

Operation Streamline

Operation Streamline is a partnership program among CBP, U.S. Attorneys, and District Court judges in certain border districts to expedite criminal justice processing. The program permits groups of up to 40 criminal defendants to have their cases heard at the same time, rather than requiring judges to review individual charges, and arranges in most cases for aliens facing felony charges for illegal re-entry to plead guilty to misdemeanor illegal entry charges—a plea bargain that leads to the rapid resolution of cases. Although Operation Streamline has been described as a zero tolerance program leading to prosecutions for 100% of apprehended aliens, the program confronts limits in judicial and detention capacity, resulting in daily caps on the number of people facing charges in certain districts. In the Tucson sector, for example, the courts reportedly limit Streamline cases to about 70 prosecutions per day.

Operation Streamline was established in the USBP's Del Rio Sector in December 2005 and expanded to the Yuma Sector in December 2006, Laredo Sector in October 2007, Tucson Sector in January 2008, and Rio Grande Valley Sector in June 2008. The program mainly consists of procedural arrangements among DHS and DOJ officials at the local level, and 15 CBP agents have been detailed to DOJ in three Border Patrol sectors to assist DOJ attorneys and U.S. Marshalls with prosecutions. A total of 208,939 people were processed through Operation Streamline through the end of FY2012—about 45% of the 463,051 immigration-related prosecutions in Southwest border districts during this period.

Sources: CBP Office of Congressional Affairs; National Research Council Committee on Estimating Costs of Immigration Enforcement in the Department of Justice, *Budgeting for Immigration Enforcement: A Path to Better Performance* (Washington, DC: National Academies Press, 2011).

- **Remote repatriation**. CBP uses a pair of programs to return Mexicans to remote locations rather than to the nearest Mexican port of entry. Under the Alien Transfer Exit Program (ATEP), certain Mexicans apprehended near the border are repatriated to border ports hundreds of miles away—typically moving people from Arizona to Texas or California—a process commonly described as "lateral repatriation."[47] Under the Mexican Interior Repatriation Program (MIRP), certain

---

(...continued)

150 million individual records. For a fuller discussion of the US-VISIT system see CRS Report R43356, *Border Security: Immigration Inspections at Ports of Entry*, by Lisa Seghetti.

[45] Aliens apprehended at the border may face federal immigration-related criminal charges for illegal entry (8 U.S.C. §1325) or (on a second or subsequent apprehension) illegal re-entry (8 U.S.C. §1326), and in some cases they may face charges related to human smuggling (8 U.S.C. §1324) and visa and document fraud (18 U.S.C. §1546), among other charges. Unlawful *presence* in the United States absent additional factors, however, is a civil violation, not a criminal offense. See CRS Report RL32480, *Immigration Consequences of Criminal Activity*, by Michael John Garcia.

[46] A total of about 3,000 people were transferred to Mexico for prosecution under the program in FY2005-FY2012, according to data provided to CRS by CBP Office of Congressional Affairs.

[47] See U.S. Congress, House Committee on Homeland Security, Subcommittee on Border and Maritime Security, *Does Administrative Amnesty Harm our Efforts to Gain and Maintain Operational Control of the Border*, testimony of U.S. Border Patrol Chief Michael J. Fisher, 112th Cong., 1st sess., October 4, 2011.

Mexican nationals are repatriated to their home towns within Mexico rather than being returned just across the border.[48]

In general, these high consequence enforcement outcomes are intended to deter illegal flows by raising the costs to migrants of being apprehended and by making it more difficult for them to reconnect with smugglers following a failed entry attempt.[49] To manage these disparate programs, CBP has designed the "Consequence Delivery System.... to uniquely evaluate each subject [who is apprehended] and identify the ideal consequences to deliver to impede and deter further illegal activity."[50] USBP agents use laminated cards with matrices describing the range of enforcement actions available for a particular alien as a function of the person's immigration and criminal histories, among other factors, and of the enforcement resources available in each Border Patrol sector. According to public comments by then CBP Commissioner Alan Bersin, the goal of the Consequence Delivery System, in certain sectors of the border, is to ensure that virtually everyone who is apprehended faces "some type of consequence" other than voluntary return.[51]

As **Figure 1** indicates, the effort to limit voluntary returns in favor of "high consequence" enforcement outcomes has, to a great degree, been implemented. The figure depicts Southwest border apprehensions (the solid line) and the four main types of enforcement outcomes (voluntary returns, criminal charges, formal removal, and remote repatriation—the shaded areas) for FY2005-FY2012. (Enforcement outcomes exceed apprehensions because some aliens face more than one outcome, such as formal removal along with lateral repatriation. In addition, certain aliens apprehended in one fiscal year do not complete their case processing until the following year.) As the figure illustrates, voluntary return fell from 77% of all enforcement outcomes in 2005 (956,470 out of 1,238,554) to 14% in FY2012 (76,664 out of 529,393). Conversely, the proportion of enforcement outcomes that were high consequence outcomes (i.e., criminal charges, formal removal, or remote repatriation) increased from 23% (282,084 out of 1,238,554) in FY2005 to 86% in FY2012 (452,664 out of 529,393).

---

[48] Ibid.

[49] See U.S. Congress, House Committee on Homeland Security, Subcommittee on Border and Maritime Security, *Does Administrative Amnesty Harm our Efforts to Gain and Maintain Operational Control of the Border*, testimony of U.S. Border Patrol Chief Michael J. Fisher, 112th Cong., 1st sess., October 4, 2011. Most alien smugglers reportedly charge aliens a set fee to enter the United States regardless of the number of attempts, so one goal of the high consequence enforcement programs is to disrupt smugglers' business model.

[50] Ibid. The Consequence Delivery System was formally launched January 1, 2011.

[51] Alan Bersin, *The State of US/Mexico Border Security*, Center for American Progress, August 4, 2011. Under section 240B of the Immigration and Nationality Act (INA), immigration officers and/or immigration judges may permit certain aliens to depart the United States in lieu of (or at the termination of) a formal removal hearing, a process known as "voluntary departure" or "voluntary return." Bersin indicated that certain aliens may still be eligible for voluntary return, such as aliens younger than 18 years old traveling without a parent or legal guardian (i.e., unaccompanied minors).

Figure 1. CBP "Enforcement with Consequences," FY2005-FY2012
Southwest Border

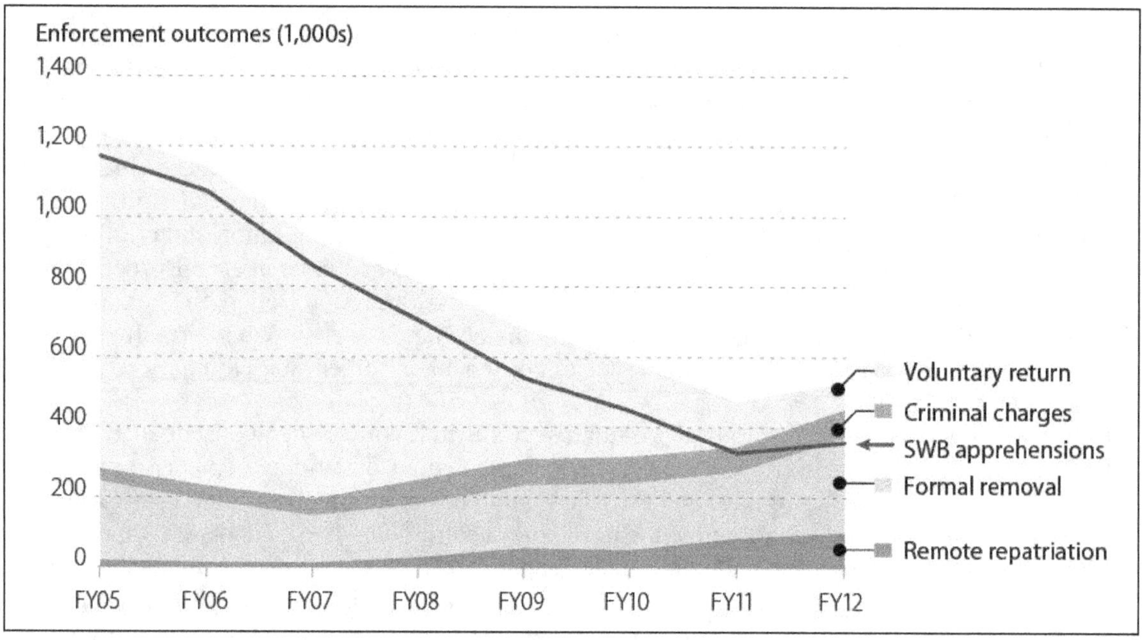

Sources: CRS presentation of data provided by CBP Office of Congressional Affairs March 10, 2013; ICE Office of Congressional Affairs March 22, 2013; Administrative Office of the U.S. Courts.

Notes: Immigration-related criminal charges may include some U.S. citizens and lawful aliens.

One factor that has facilitated the rise in the proportion of apprehensions subject to high-consequence enforcement has been a sharp drop in the number of aliens apprehended on the Southwest border, as discussed in this report (see "Alien Apprehensions"). Nonetheless, as **Figure 1** also illustrates, CBP's effort to expand high-consequence enforcement has resulted in an *absolute* rise in removals, prosecutions, and lateral/interior repatriations since 2007, even during a period of falling border apprehensions.

With the implementation of the Consequence Delivery System, the Border Patrol has initiated a new system to estimate the deterrent effect of different enforcement outcomes. In particular, USBP tracks, for each of 10 different enforcement consequences, the percentage of aliens who were re-apprehended during the same fiscal year following repatriation (i.e., the recidivism rate). These recidivism rates are reported in **Table 1**.

Table 1. Consequence Delivery System Outcomes and Recidivism Rates
Southwest Border

	Consequence	FY2011		FY2012	
		Number of Cases	Recidivism Rate	Number of Cases	Recidivism Rate
Criminal Charges	OASISS	533	14.7%	429	10.2%
	Operation Streamline	36,871	12.1%	44,300	10.3%
	Standard Prosecution	31,130	9.1%	34,839	9.1%

Consequence		FY2011		FY2012	
		Number of Cases	Recidivism Rate	Number of Cases	Recidivism Rate
Formal Removal	Notice to Appear	20,923	6.6%	23,491	3.8%
	Expedited Removal	39,855	16.6%	148,548	16.4%
	Reinstatement	74,106	16.9%	98,424	15.9%
	Quick Court	2,730	19.0%	1,070	18.3%
Remote Repatriation	MIRP	8,940	9.3%	0	NAª
	ATEP	75,966	27.8%	101,992	23.8%
Voluntary Return		129,207	29.4%	76,664	27.1%
Total Cases		**318,883**	**19.8%**	**347,921**	**16.7%**

Source: CRS analysis based on data provided by CBP Office of Congressional Affairs, March 10, 2013.

Notes: OASISS stands for the U.S.-Mexican Operation Against Smugglers Initiative on Safety and Security. See text for discussions of Operation Streamline, expedited removal, and reinstatement of removal. Standard Prosecution refers to criminal charges through the standard federal prosecution process. Notice to appear is the first stage in the standard formal removal process before an immigration judge. Quick court is a program involving expedited removal hearings before an immigration judge. MIRP stands for the Mexico Interior Repatriation Program. ATEP stands for the Alien Transfer Exchange Program. Total Cases refers to the total number of apprehensions and border-wide overall recidivism rate. The sum of the consequences exceeds the number of total cases because some people are subject to more than one consequence.

a.   MIRP did not operate in FY2012.

As **Table 1** indicates, several consequences were associated with recidivism rates well *below* the overall FY2012 average of 16.7%. These low recidivism consequences included standard removal proceedings following a notice to appear (3.8%), standard criminal prosecutions (9.1%), criminal charges through the OASISS program (10.2%), and Operation Streamline (10.3%). Recidivism rates were also lower than the FY2011 average of 19.8% for aliens returned to Mexico through the MIRP program (9.3%) in that year. (MIRP did not operate in FY2012.) Conversely, recidivism rates in FY2012 were well *above* the overall average for aliens subject to voluntary return (27.1%) and for aliens subject to lateral repatriation through the ATEP program (23.8%).

The differences in recidivism rates may not be wholly attributable to differences among the consequences because the Border Patrol takes account of aliens' migration histories and other factors when assigning people to different enforcement outcomes. Nonetheless, these data suggest that standard removal and criminal charges have a stronger deterrent effect on future unauthorized migration than does voluntary return. Conversely, lateral repatriation appears to do little to discourage people from reentering the United States.[52]

---

[52] According to CBP Office of Congressional Affairs (April 24, 2013), aliens repatriated through the Alien Transfer Exit Program (ATEP) typically are voluntarily returned or subject to expedited removal. Thus, ATEP's high recidivism rates are partly a result of the relatively high rates associated with these two outcomes.

Budget and Resources

Statutory and strategic changes since 1986 are reflected in border enforcement appropriations and in CBP's assets at the border, including personnel, infrastructure, and surveillance technology. This section reviews trends in each of these areas.

Border Security Appropriations

Figure 2 depicts U.S. Border Patrol appropriations for FY1989-FY2013. Appropriations have grown steadily over this period, rising from $232 million in 1989 to $1.3 billion in FY2002 (the last data available prior to the creation of DHS), $3.8 billion in FY2010, and $3.7 billion in FY2013—a nominal increase of 1,450% and an increase of 730% when accounting for inflation.[53] The largest growth came following the formation of DHS in FY2003, reflecting Congress's focus on border security in the aftermath of 9/11.

Figure 2. U.S. Border Patrol Appropriations, FY1989-FY2013

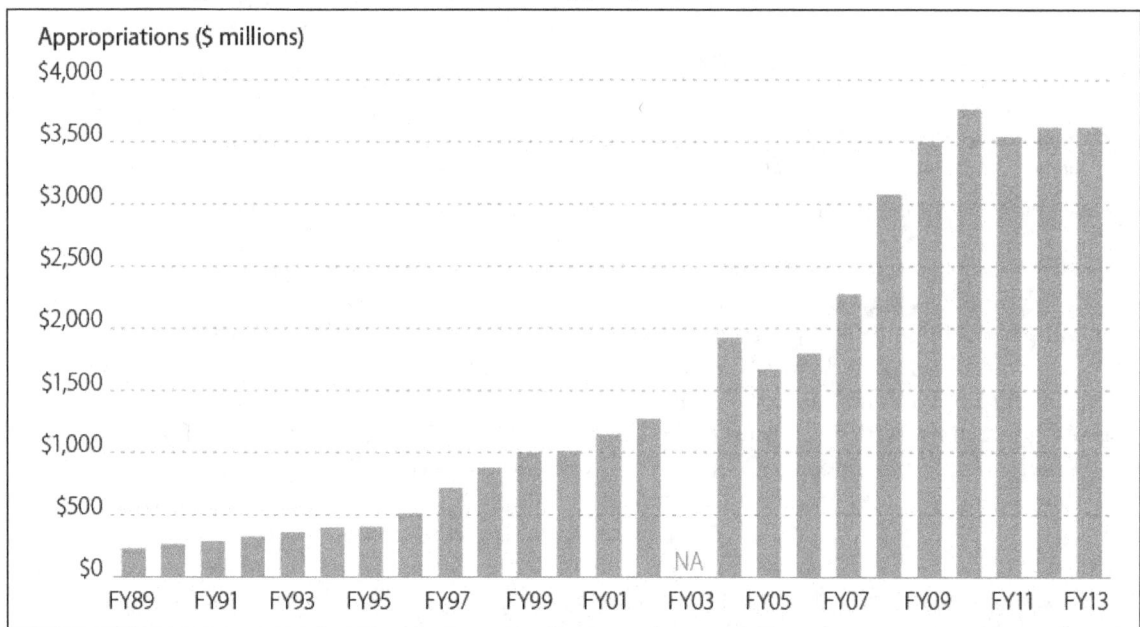

Sources: INS Congressional Budget Justification FY1991-FY2002; DHS Appropriations reports FY2004-FY2013.

Notes: Appropriations for 1989-2002 reflect the "Border Patrol" sub-account of the INS Salaries and Expenses account of the DOJ annual appropriations. Appropriations for 2004-2013 reflect the "Border Security and Control between Ports of Entry" sub-account of the CBP Salaries and Expenses account of the DHS annual appropriations. Data are not available for FY2003 because neither the INS nor congressional appropriators provided a breakout of the salaries and expenses sub-accounts within the Enforcement and Border Affairs account during that year's funding cycle. The overall Enforcement and Border Affairs account within INS for

---

[53] See **Figure 2** for sources. Due to the manner in which the Border Patrol collects and organizes its data, all statistics presented in this report (except where otherwise indicated) are based on the federal fiscal year, which begins October 1 and ends on September 30. All dollar amounts in this report are nominal values for the year from which data are reported, with adjustments for inflation here and below based on CRS calculations using Bureau of Labor Statistics, "CPI Inflation Calculator," http://data.bls.gov/cgi-bin/cpicalc.pl.

FY2003 was $2,881 million, up from $2,541 million in FY2001 and $2,740 million in FY2002. With the establishment of DHS, the former INS, customs inspections from the former U.S. Customs Service, and the U.S. Border Patrol were merged to form the Bureau of Customs and Border Protection within DHS. As a result, data for years prior to FY2003 may not be strictly comparable with data for FY2004 and after. FY2005 figure includes a $124 million supplemental appropriation from P.L. 109-13. FY2006 figure does not include any portion of the $423 million in supplemental funding for CBP Salaries and Expenses in P.L. 109-234 because the law did not specify how much of this funding was for USBP; DHS reported in its FY2008 DHS Budget Justification that the Border Patrol received a $1,900 million appropriation in FY2006. FY2010 figure includes a $176 million supplemental appropriation from P.L. 111-230.

Appropriations reported in **Figure 2** are only a *subset* of all border security funding. These data do not include, for example, additional CBP sub-accounts funding Headquarters Management and Administration ($1.4 billion in FY2013), and Border Security Inspections and Trade Facilitation at Ports of Entry ($3.2 billion); or additional CBP accounts funding Border Security Fencing, Infrastructure, and Technology ($324 million); Air and Marine Operations ($799 million) and Construction and Facilities Management ($234 million).[54] A substantial portion of these accounts is dedicated to border security and immigration enforcement, as these terms are commonly used. The data in **Figure 2** also exclude U.S. Immigration and Customs Enforcement (ICE) appropriations, which totaled $5.4 billion for Salaries and Expenses for FY2013.[55] About a quarter of ICE's 20,000 personnel reportedly are deployed to the Southwest border.[56] And **Figure 2** excludes border enforcement appropriations for other federal agencies—including the Departments of Justice, Defense, the Interior, and Agriculture, all of which play a role in border security—as well as funding for the U.S. federal court system.[57]

Border Patrol Personnel

Accompanying this budget increase, Congress has passed at least four laws since 1986 authorizing increased Border Patrol personnel.[58] USBP staffing roughly doubled in the decade after the 1986 IRCA, doubled again between 1996 and the 9/11 attacks, and doubled again in the decade after 9/11 (see **Figure 3**). As of January 2013, the USBP had 21,370 agents, including 18,462 posted at the Southwest border and 2,212 posted at the northern border.[59] These numbers

---

[54] Account-level data are from the House Explanatory Statement to accompany P.L. 113-6. Also see CRS Report R42644, *Department of Homeland Security: FY2013 Appropriations*, coordinated by William L. Painter.

[55] Ibid.

[56] Department of Homeland Security, "Secure and Manage Our Borders," http://www.dhs.gov/xabout/gc_1240606351110.shtm.

[57] Over one-third of all federal criminal cases commenced in 2011-12 were for immigration cases; see U.S. Courts, *U.S. District Courts - Criminal Cases Commenced, by Offense*, Washington, DC, 2011, http://www.uscourts.gov/uscourts/Statistics/JudicialBusiness/2012/appendices/D02DSep12.pdf. The prosecution of these cases involves expenditures by DOJ prosecutors, federal marshals, the federal bureau of prisons, and the U.S. district and magistrate court systems, among others. The costs of border enforcement borne by federal law enforcement and judicial officials outside of DHS are difficult to describe because these agencies do not list border-specific obligations in their budget documents. Also see National Research Council Committee on Estimating Costs of Immigration Enforcement in the Department of Justice, op. cit.

[58] The Immigration Act of 1990 (P.L. 101-649) authorized an increase of 1,000 Border Patrol agents; the IIRIRA (P.L. 104-208, Div. C) authorized an increase of a total of 5,000 Border Patrol agents in FY1997-FY2001; the Uniting and Strengthening America by Providing Appropriate Tools Required to Intercept and Obstruct Terrorism Act (USA PATRIOT, P.L. 107-56) authorized INS to triple the number of Border Patrol agents at the northern border; and the Intelligence Reform and Terrorism Prevention Act (P.L. 108-458) authorized an increase of 10,000 Border Patrol agents between FY2006 and FY2010.

[59] CBP Office of Congressional Affairs, January 9, 2013.

are up from a total of 2,268 Border Patrol agents in 1980 (including 1,975 at the Southwest border and 211 at the northern border) and 10,045 in 2002 (including 9,239 at the Southwest border and 492 at the northern border).[60]

Figure 3. U.S. Border Patrol Agents, Total and by Region, FY1980-FY2013

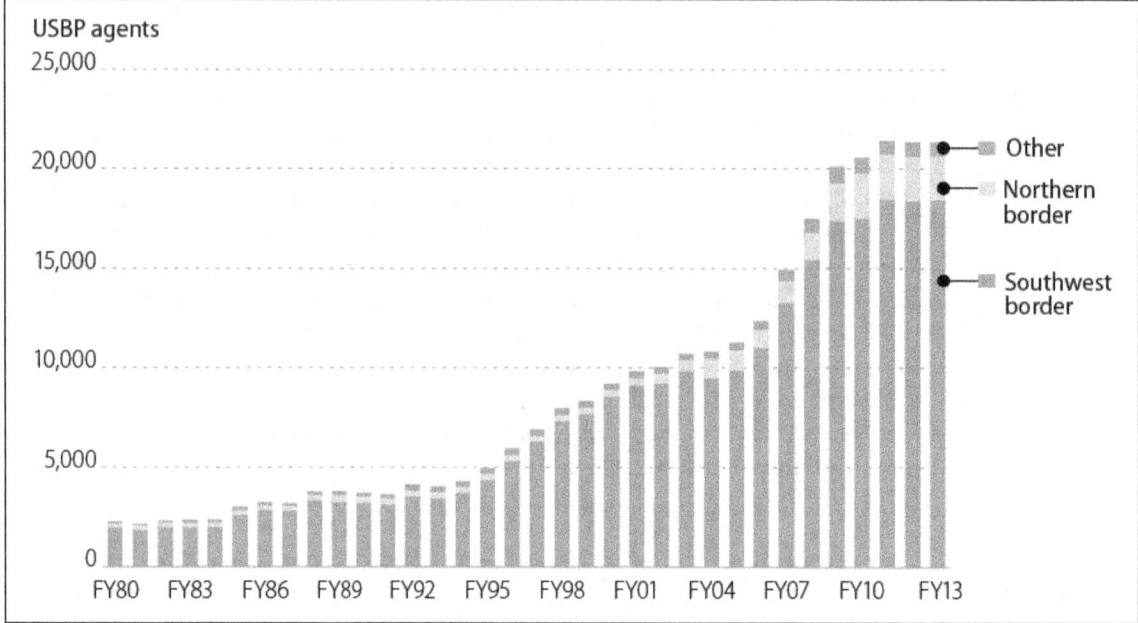

Source: 1980-1991: CRS presentation of data from Syracuse University Transactional Records Access Clearinghouse; 1992-2011: CRS presentation of data provided by CBP Office of Congressional Affairs.

Note: The total number of Border Patrol agents includes agents stationed in coastal sectors and at USBP headquarters.

National Guard Troops at the Border

The National Guard also is authorized to support federal, state, and local law enforcement agencies (LEAs) at the border. Basic authority for the Department of Defense (DOD, including the National Guard) to assist LEAs is contained in Chapter 18 of Title 10 of the U.S. Code, and DOD personnel are expressly authorized to maintain and operate equipment in cooperation with federal LEAs in conjunction with the enforcement of counterterrorism operations or the enforcement of counterdrug laws, immigration laws, and customs requirements.[61] DOD may assist any federal, state, or local LEA requesting counterdrug assistance under the National Defense Authorization Act, as amended.[62] Under Title 32 of the U.S. Code, National Guard personnel also may serve a federal purpose, such as border security, and receive federal pay while remaining under the command control of their respective state governors.[63]

---

[60] See sources cited in **Figure 3**.

[61] See CRS Report R41286, *Securing America's Borders: The Role of the Military*, by R. Chuck Mason.

[62] P.L. 101-510. Div. A, Title X, §1004; also see Ibid.

[63] 32 U.S.C. §§502(a) and 502(f); also see CRS Report R41286, *Securing America's Borders: The Role of the Military*, by R. Chuck Mason.

National Guard troops were first deployed to the border on a pilot basis in 1988, when about 100 soldiers assisted the U.S. Customs Service at several Southwest border locations, and National Guard and active military units provided targeted support for the USBP's surveillance programs throughout the following decade. The first large-scale deployment of the National Guard to the border occurred in 2006-2008, when over 30,000 troops provided engineering, aviation, identification, technical, logistical, and administrative support to CBP as part of "Operation Jump Start."[64] President Obama announced an additional deployment of up to 1,200 National Guard troops to the Southwest border on May 25, 2010, with the National Guard supporting the Border Patrol, by providing intelligence work and drug and human trafficking interdiction.[65] The 2010 deployment was originally scheduled to end in June 2011, but the full deployment was extended twice (in June and September 2011). The Administration announced in December 2011 that the deployment would be reduced to fewer than 300 troops beginning in January 2012, with National Guard efforts focused on supporting DHS's aerial surveillance operations.[66] In December 2012, DHS and the Department of Defense announced that the National Guard deployment would be extended through December 2013.[67]

Fencing and Tactical Infrastructure

Border tactical infrastructure includes roads, lighting, pedestrian fencing, and vehicle barriers. Tactical infrastructure is intended to impede illicit cross-border activity, disrupt and restrict smuggling operations, and establish a substantial probability of apprehending terrorists seeking entry into the United States.[68] The former INS installed the first fencing along the U.S.-Mexican border beginning in 1990 east of the Pacific Ocean near San Diego.

Congress expressly authorized the construction and improvement of fencing and other barriers under Section 102(a) of the Illegal Immigration Reform and Immigrant Responsibility Act of 1996 (IIRIRA; P.L. 104-208, Div. C), which also required (pursuant to Section 102(b)) the completion of a triple-layered fence along the original 14 mile border segment near San Diego. The Secure Fence Act of 2006 (P.L. 109-367) amended IIRIRA Section 102(b) with a requirement for double-layered fencing along five segments of the Southwest border, totaling about 850 miles.[69] IIRIRA was amended again by the Consolidated Appropriations Act, FY2008 (P.L. 110-161). Under that amendment, the law now requires the Secretary of Homeland Security to construct reinforced fencing "along not less than 700 miles of the southwest border where fencing would be most practical and effective and provide for the installation of additional physical barriers, roads, lighting, cameras, and sensors to gain operational control of the southwest border."[70] The act further specifies, however, that the Secretary of Homeland Security is *not*

---

[64] See CRS Report R41286, *Securing America's Borders: The Role of the Military*, by R. Chuck Mason.

[65] Ibid.

[66] Associated Press, "National Guard Troops at Mexico Border Cut to Fewer Than 300," *USA Today*, December 20, 2011.

[67] Homeland Security Today, "Pentagon Extends Deployment of National Guard in CBP Air Support Mission," December 7, 2012.

[68] Customs and Border Protection, "Tactical Infrastructure: History and Purpose," http://www.cbp.gov/xp/cgov/border_security/ti/about_ti/ti_history xml.

[69] P.L. 109-367 identified five specific stretches of the border where fencing was to be installed; CBP Congressional Affairs provided CRS with this estimate of the total mileage covered by the law on September 25, 2006.

[70] P.L. 110-161, Div. E, §564. Unlike under prior law, the Consolidated Appropriations Act, as enacted, does not specify that reinforced fencing be "at least 2 layers." See P.L. 104-208, Div. C, §102(b), as amended by P.L. 109-367, (continued...)

required to install fencing "in a particular location along the international border of the United States if the Secretary determines that the use or placement of such resources is not the most appropriate means to achieve and maintain operational control over the international border at such location."[71]

Figure 4. Tactical Infrastructure Appropriations and Miles of Border Fencing, FY1996-FY2012

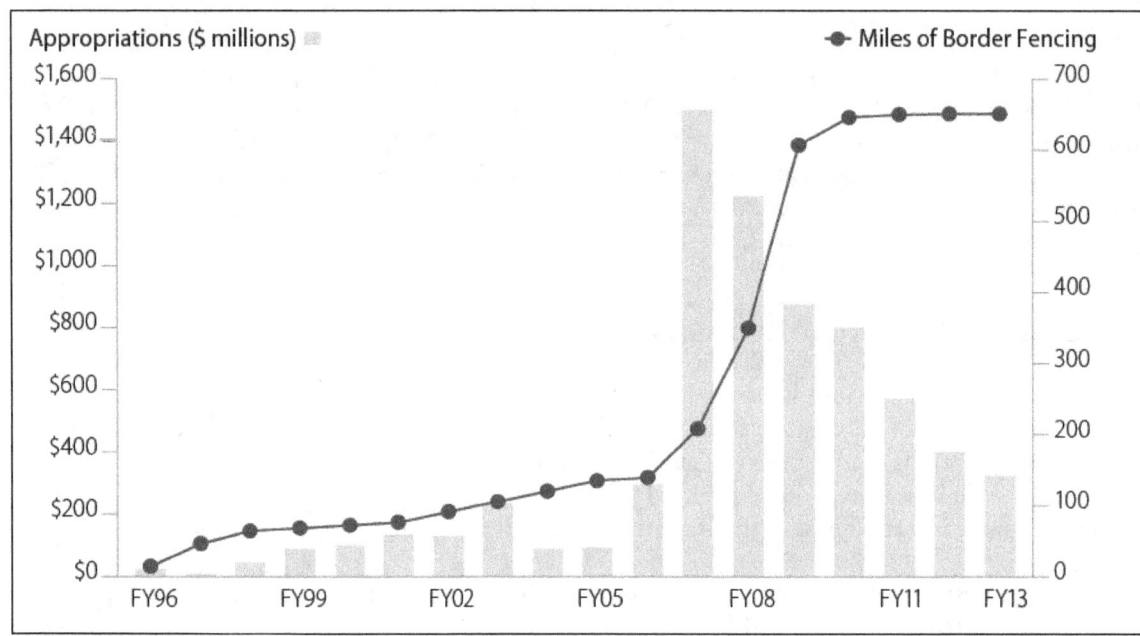

Sources: INS Congressional Budget Justifications FY2001-FY2003; DHS Congressional Budget Justifications FY2005-2007; DHS Appropriations bills FY2007-FY2013.

Notes: In FY2003, immigration inspections from the former INS, customs inspections from the former U.S. Customs Service, and USBP were merged to form the Bureau of Customs and Border Protection within DHS. As a result, data for years prior to FY2003 may not be comparable with the data for FY2004 and after. Data for FY1996-FY2002 include USBP construction and tactical infrastructure accounts. Construction account funding has been used to fund a number of projects at the border, including fencing, vehicle barriers, roads, and USBP stations and checkpoints. Funding for FY1998-FY2000 includes San Diego fencing as well as fencing, light, and road projects in El Centro, Tucson, El Paso, and Marfa. Data for FY2003-FY2006 include DHS construction and tactical appropriations. Data for FY2007-FY2012 include total appropriations to CBP's Border Security Fencing, Infrastructure, and Technology (BSFIT) account. This account funds the construction of fencing, other infrastructure such as roads and vehicle barriers, as well as border technologies such as cameras and sensors.

As of January 15, 2013, DHS had installed 352 miles of primary pedestrian fencing, 299 miles of vehicle fencing (total of 651 miles), and 36 miles of secondary fencing (see **Figure 4**). The Border Patrol reportedly had identified a total of 653 miles of the border as appropriate for fencing and barriers (i.e., 2 additional miles).[72] **Figure 4** also summarizes annual appropriations for tactical infrastructure (including surveillance technology) for FY1996-FY2013.

(...continued)

§3.

[71] P.L. 110-161, Div. E, §564.

[72] Testimony of DHS Secretary Janet Napolitano before the Senate Judiciary Committee, *The Border Security, Economic Opportunity, and Immigration Modernization Act, S. 744*, 113th Cong., 1st sess., April 23, 2013.

Appropriations increased from $25 million in FY1996 to $298 million in FY2006, an 11-fold increase (8-fold when adjusting for inflation), and then jumped to $1.5 billion in FY2007 as DHS created a new Border Security Fencing, Infrastructure, and Technology (BSFIT) account and appropriated money to pay for the border fencing mandate in the Secure Fence Act of 2006. BSFIT appropriations have fallen every year since FY2007, reaching $324 million in FY2013.

Surveillance Assets

The Border Patrol uses advanced technology to augment its agents' ability to patrol the border. USBP's border surveillance system has its origins in the former Immigration and Naturalization Service's (INS's) Integrated Surveillance Information System (ISIS), initiated in 1998. ISIS was folded into a broader border surveillance system named the America's Shield Initiative (ASI) in 2005, and ASI was made part of DHS's Secure Border Initiative (SBI) the following year, with the surveillance program renamed SBI*net* and managed under contract by the Boeing Corporation.

Under all three of these names, the system consisted of a network of remote video surveillance (RVS) systems (including cameras and infrared systems), and sensors (including seismic, magnetic, and thermal detectors), linked into a computer network, known as the Integrated Computer Assisted Detection (ICAD) database. The system was intended to ensure seamless coverage of the border by combining the feeds from multiple cameras and sensors into one remote-controlled system linked to a central communications control room at a USBP station or sector headquarters. USBP personnel monitoring the control room screened the ICAD system to re-position RVS cameras toward the location where sensor alarms were tripped. Control room personnel then alerted field agents to the intrusion and coordinated the response.

All three of these systems struggled to meet deployment timelines and to provide USBP with the promised level of border surveillance.[73] DHS also faced criticism of ASI and SBI*net* for non-competitive contracting practices, inadequate oversight of contractors, and cost overruns.[74] DHS Secretary Napolitano ordered a department-wide assessment of the SBI*net* technology project in January 2010 and suspended the SBI*net* contract in March 2010.[75] The review confirmed SBI*net*'s history of "continued and repeated technical problems, cost overruns, and schedule delays, raising serious questions about the system's ability to meet the needs for technology along the border."[76] DHS terminated SBI*net* in January 2011.

---

[73] See, for example, testimony of DHS Inspector General Richard L. Skinner before the House Homeland Security Committee, Subcommittee on Management, Integration, and Oversight, *New Secure Border Initiative*, 109th Cong., 1st sess., December 16, 2005; GAO, *Secure Border Initiative: DHS Needs to Address Significant Risks in Delivering Key Technology Investment*, GAO-08-1086, September 22, 2008; and GAO, Secure *Border Initiative: Technology Deployment Delays Persist and the Impact of Border Fencing Has Not Been Assessed,* GAO-09-896, http://www.gao.gov/new.items/d09896.pdf.

[74] See DHS Inspector General (DHS IG), *Secure Border Initiative: DHS Needs to Address Significant Risks in Delivering Key Technology Investment*, DHS OIG-09-80, Washington, DC, June 2009; DHS IG, *Controls Over SBInet Program Cost and Schedule Could Be Improved*, DHS OIG-10-96, Washington, DC, June 2010.

[75] Testimony of CBP Assistant Commissioner Mark Borkowski before the House Committee on Homeland Security, Subcommittee on Border and Maritime Security, *After SBInet–The Future of Technology on the Border*, 112th Cong., 1st sess., March 15, 2011.

[76] DHS, *Report on the Assessment of the Secure Border Initiative Network (SBI*net*) Program*, Washington, DC, 2010, p. 1.

Under the department's current Arizona Surveillance Technology Plan, the Border Patrol deploys a mix of different surveillance technologies designed to meet the specific needs of different border regions. As of November 2012, deployed assets included 337 Remote Video Surveillance Systems (RVSS) consisting of fixed daylight and infrared cameras that transmit images to a central location (up from 269 in 2006), 198 short and medium range Mobile Vehicle Surveillance Systems (MVSS) mounted on trucks and monitored in the truck's passenger compartment (up from zero in 2005) and 41 long range Mobile Surveillance Systems (MSS, up from zero in 2005), 12 hand-held agent portable medium range surveillance systems (APSS, up from zero in 2005), 15 Integrated Fixed Towers that were developed as part of the SBInet system (up from zero in 2005), and 13,406 unattended ground sensors (up from about 11,200 in 2005).[77] According to CBP officials, the department's acquisitions strategy emphasizes flexible equipment and mobile technology that permits USBP to surge surveillance capacity in a particular region, and off-the-shelf technology in order to hold down costs and get resources on the ground more quickly.

Aerial and Marine Surveillance

In addition to these ground-based surveillance assets, CBP deploys manned and unmanned aircraft as well as marine vessels to conduct surveillance. Air and marine vessels patrol regions of the border that are inaccessible to other surveillance assets, with unmanned aerial systems (UAS) deployed in areas considered too high-risk for manned aircraft or personnel on the ground.[78] In FY2012, CBP's Office of Air and Marine deployed 19 types of aircraft and three classes of marine vessels, for a total of 269 aircraft and 293 marine vessels operating from over 70 locations.[79] The agency reported 81,045 flight hours (down from about 95,000 in FY2011) and 47,742 underway hours in marine vessels (down from about 133,000 in FY2011).[80] As of November 2012, CBP operated a total of 10 UAS up from zero in 2006, including 2 UAS on the Northern border, 5 on the Southwest border, and 3 in the Gulf of Mexico.[81] UAS accounted for 5,737 flight hours in FY2012, up from 4,406 hours in FY2011.[82]

With support from Department of Defense (DOD), CBP conducted an evaluation of two unmanned aerostat (tethered blimp) systems during the summer of 2012: the Persistent Ground Surveillance System (PGSS) and the Rapid Aerostat Initial Deployment (RAID). In addition, CBP evaluated PGSS and RAID towers, which support aerostat deployment as well as ground-based technologies. These two systems have been deployed by the military to conduct area surveillance. As a result of the evaluation, CBP concluded that these systems could provide useful

---

[77] 2012 data from U.S. Border Patrol Office of Congressional Affairs November 8, 2012; FY2006 data from DHS Congressional Budget Justification 2006; 2005 data from GAO, "Border Security: Key Unresolved Issues Justify Reevaluation of Border Surveillance Technology Program," GAO-06-295, February 2006.

[78] U.S. Congress, Senate Committee on the Judiciary, *The Future of Drones in America: Law Enforcement and Privacy Considerations*, testimony of DHS Acting Officer for Civil Rights and Civil Liberties Tamara Kessler, 113th Congress, 1st sess., March 20, 2013.

[79] CBP Office of Congressional Affairs, March 19, 2013.

[80] Ibid.; and CBP Office of Air and Marine, 2011 Air and Marine Milestones and Achievements," http://www.cbp.gov/xp/cgov/border_security/am/operations/2011_achiev xml.

[81] Northern border UAS are based in Grand Forks, ND; Southwest border UAS are based in Sierra Vista, AZ (four systems) and Corpus Christi, TX (one system); and maritime UAS are based in Corpus Christi, TX (one system) and in Cape Canaveral, FL (two systems).

[82] Ibid.

---

support to CBP operations on the border; and CBP reportedly is working with DOD to identify opportunities to transfer ownership of aerostats returning from overseas to CBP.[83]

Border Patrol Enforcement Data

For 90 years, the Border Patrol has recorded the number of deportable aliens apprehended in the United States;[84] and alien apprehensions remain the agency's primary indicator of immigration enforcement. The agency also collects several additional measures of immigration enforcement, including unique apprehensions, alien recidivism, and estimated turn backs and got aways. These enforcement outcomes provide insight into the state of the border, as discussed in this section, but they confront certain limitations when it comes to estimating illegal border inflows (see "Metrics of Border Security").

Alien Apprehensions

Figure 5 depicts total USBP apprehensions of deportable and removable aliens for FY1960-FY2012. Apprehensions are widely understood to be correlated with illegal flows, and the data in **Figure 5** reflect historical trends in unauthorized migration (see "Border Patrol History and Strategy"). Thus, apprehensions were very low in the 1960s, but climbed sharply in the two decades after 1965. Apprehensions reached an all-time high of 1.7 million in 1986 and again in 2000, and an average of more than 1.2 million apprehensions per year were recorded 1983-2006, reflecting high levels of unauthorized migration throughout this period. As **Figure 5** also illustrates, apprehensions have fallen sharply since 2000, and particularly since 2006. The 340,252 apprehensions observed in 2011 were the lowest level since 1971, and the 364,768 apprehensions in 2012 were the second-lowest level since that time. Falling apprehensions likely reflect fewer illegal inflows since 2006, though the degree to which reduced inflows are a result of effective enforcement versus other factors like the recent U.S. economic downturn remains subject to debate (see "How Secure is the U.S. Border?").

---

[83] CBP Office of Congressional Affairs, March 21, 2013.

[84] Deportable aliens located refer to Border Patrol apprehensions and ICE administrative arrests. Prior to 1952, data refer to Border Patrol apprehensions.

Figure 5. Total USBP Apprehensions of Deportable Aliens, FY1960-FY2012

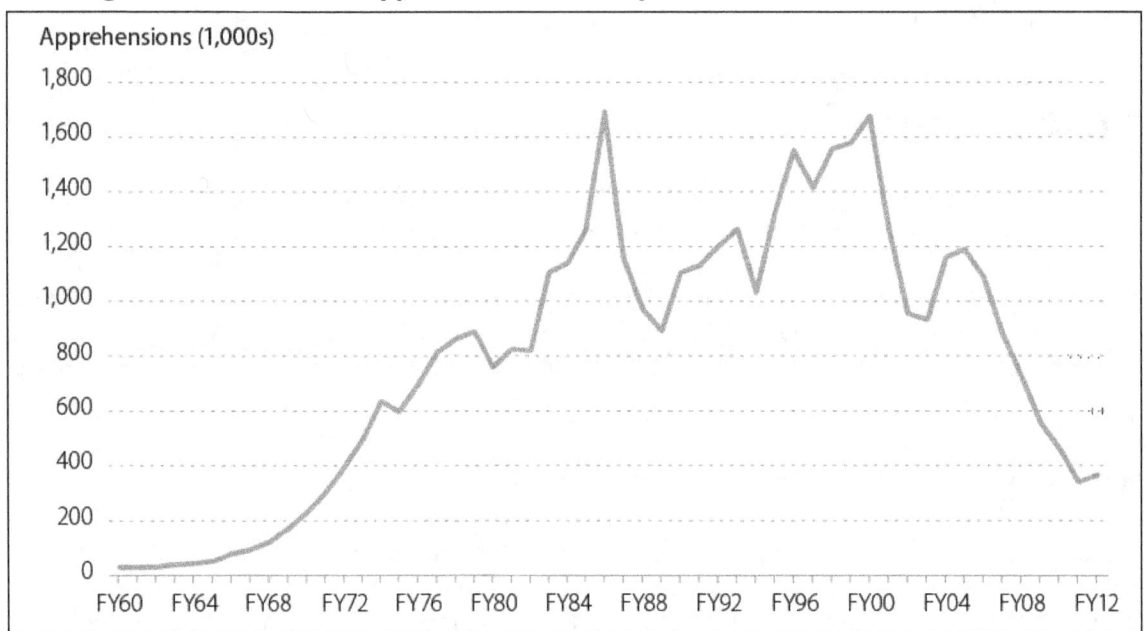

Source: U.S. Border Patrol.

Southwest Border Apprehensions by Sector

Figure 6 depicts apprehensions along the Southwest border for FY1992-FY2012, broken down by certain Border Patrol sectors. The sector-specific apprehension pattern generally adheres to the predictions of the 1994 National Strategic Plan. Increased enforcement in the El Paso and San Diego sectors was associated with high apprehensions in those sectors during the early 1990s, and then with falling apprehensions by the middle of the decade. Apprehensions in the San Diego and El Paso sectors remained well below their early-1990s levels throughout the following decade—findings that suggest border enforcement in those sectors has been broadly effective.

Figure 6. U.S. Border Patrol Apprehensions of Deportable Aliens, Southwest Border, by Selected Sectors, FY1992-FY2012

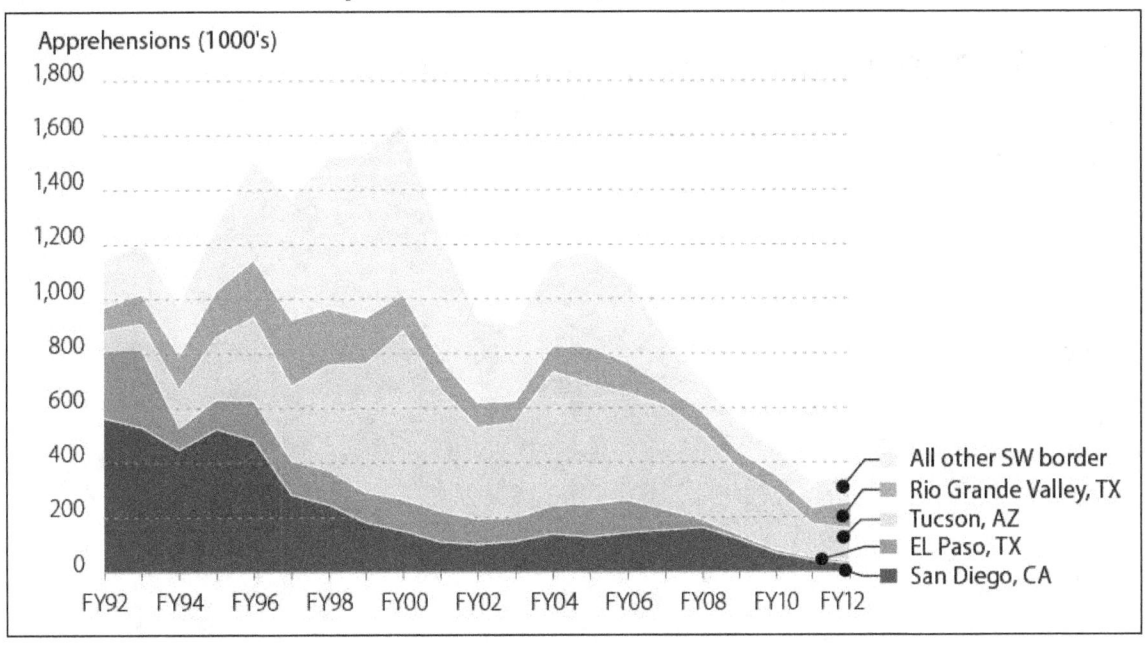

Source: USBP, Total Apprehensions by Southwest Border Sectors.

Falling apprehensions in San Diego and El Paso during the late 1990s initially were more than offset by rising apprehensions in the Tucson, AZ, sector and other border locations, including the Laredo and Del Rio, TX, sectors. Since FY2011, apprehensions in Tucson have fallen back to their lowest level since 1993, but apprehensions in the Rio Grande Valley have increased, and now account for more than a quarter of Southwest border apprehensions.[85] Thus, since the initiation of the prevention through deterrence approach in the mid-1990s, it appears that success in San Diego and El Paso may have come at the expense of Tucson and other sectors.

Unique Subjects and Alien Recidivism

Overall apprehensions data record apprehension *events*, and therefore count certain individuals more than once because they enter and are apprehended multiple times. Since 2000, the Border Patrol also has tracked the number of *unique subjects* the agency apprehends per year by analyzing biometric data (i.e., fingerprints and digital photographs) of persons apprehended.[86] As **Figure 7** illustrates, trends in unique subjects apprehended are similar to total apprehensions:

---

[85] Also see Adam Isacson and Maureen Meyer, "Border Security and Migration: A Report from South Texas," *Washington Office on Latin America*, http://www.wola.org/sites/default/files/downloadable/Mexico/2013/Border%20Security%20and%20Migration%20South%20Texas.pdf.

[86] Biometric data of persons apprehended are recorded in the Automated Biometric Identification System (IDENT) system. When Border Patrol agents enter aliens' biometric data in the IDENT system, the data are automatically checked against DHS' "recidivist" database, which is used to track repeat entrants, and its "lookout" database, which is used to identify criminal aliens. US-VISIT workstations also are fully interoperable with the Federal Bureau of Investigation's (FBI) 10-print Integrated Automated Fingerprint Identification System (IAFIS), a biometric database that includes data on criminal records and the Department of Defense's (DOD) Automated Biometric Identification System (ABIS), which contains national security data.

falling from 2000-2003, climbing in 2004-2005, and then falling sharply from about 818,000 in 2005 to about 247,000 individuals in 2011, before climbing back to 284,000 in FY2012.

Figure 7. USBP Southwest Border Unique Subjects and Recidivism Rates
FY2000-FY2012

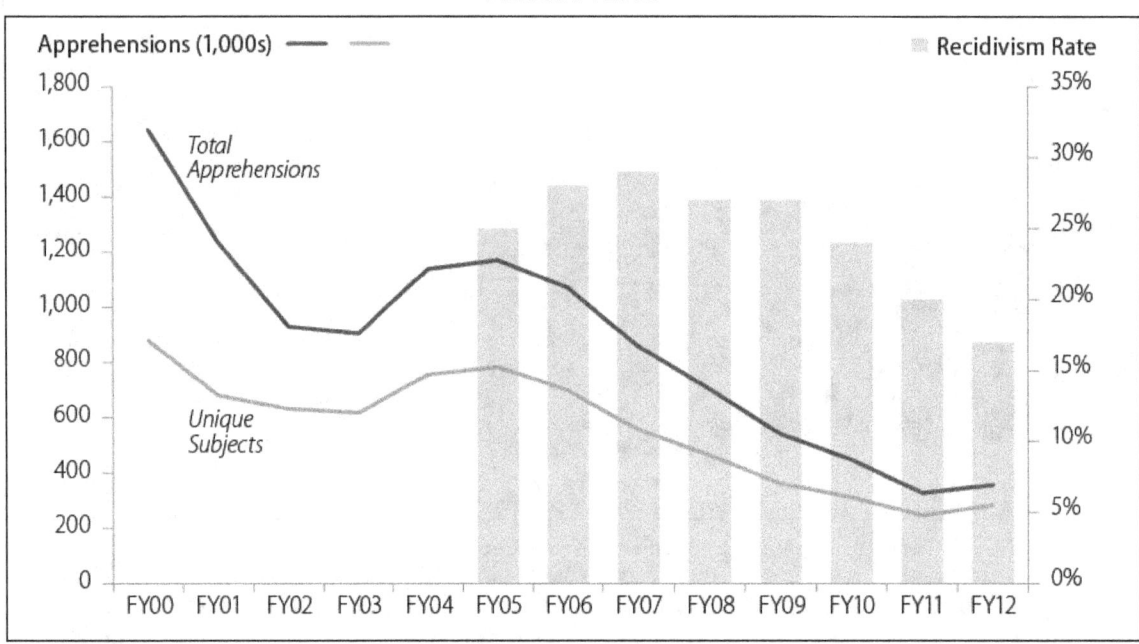

Source: CRS presentation of data provided by CBP Office of Congressional Affairs, March 10, 2013.

Notes: Total apprehensions refer to the total number of USBP apprehensions in Southwest border sectors; *unique subjects* refers to the number of different people apprehended based on biometric records. The recidivism rate is the percentage of unique individuals apprehended two or more times in a given fiscal year.

Significantly, the gap between total and unique apprehensions has steadily narrowed, with unique subjects representing 54%-55% of total apprehensions in 2000-2001, 65%-70% in 2002-2010, and 75%-80% in 2011-2012. Put another way, each unique subject is being apprehended fewer times, on average, with the aggregate average number of apprehensions per person apprehended (i.e., total apprehensions divided by unique subjects) falling from 1.9 apprehensions per person in 2000 to 1.3 apprehensions per person in 2012.[87]

This trend is explained, in part, by the bars in **Figure 7**, which depict annual Southwest border recidivism rates, which USBP has tracked since 2005. The Border Patrol defines the annual recidivism rate as the percentage of unique subjects apprehended more than once in a given fiscal year. A goal of the Consequence Delivery System has been to deter aliens from re-entering—that is, to reduce recidivism. As **Figure 7** illustrates, recidivism rates increased slightly between 2005 (25%) and 2007 (29%), but have fallen since that time, reaching 17% in 2012.

---

[87] These calculations are based on aggregate data provided to CRS.

Estimated "Got Aways" and "Turn Backs"

Border Patrol stations and sectors estimate the number of illegal entrants who successfully travel to the U.S. interior and who USBP ceased pursuing, or "got aways."[88] Stations and sectors also estimate "turn backs," the number of people who illegally cross the border but then cross back to Mexico. USBP uses the sum of got aways, turn backs, and apprehensions to estimate *the total number of known illegal entries* (also see "Border Patrol Effectiveness Rate"). The agency has used these data since 2006 to inform tactical decision making and to allocate resources across Southwest border sectors, but the Border Patrol has not published them or viewed them as reliable metrics of border security because of challenges associated with measuring got aways and turn backs across different border sectors.[89]

Additional Border Security Data: Migrant Surveys

Apart from Border Patrol data on enforcement outcomes, a second major source of information about unauthorized migration and border security is survey data based on interviews with migrants and potential migrants. Much of the research on unauthorized migration across the Southwest border focuses on Mexicans because Mexico historically accounts for about 95% of persons apprehended at the Southwest border.[90] An advantage to surveys is that they may collect more information about their subjects than is found in enforcement data. In addition, because surveys are conducted within the U.S. interior as well as in migrant countries of origin (i.e., Mexico), surveys may capture more information about successful illegal inflows and about the deterrent effects of enforcement. In 2011, DHS commissioned a comprehensive study by the National Research Council (NRC) on the use of surveys and related methodologies to estimate the number of illegal U.S.-Mexico border crossings; and the NRC recommended that DHS use survey data along with enforcement data to measure illegal flows and the effectiveness of border enforcement.[91]

Two binational (U.S.-Mexican) surveys may be particularly useful for estimating illegal flows because they have examined migration dynamics in migrant-sending and –receiving communities for a number of years. The surveys are the Mexican Migration Field Research Program (MMFRP) based at the University of California-San Diego (UCSD) and the Mexican Migration Project (MMP) based at Princeton University. These targeted surveys ask a number of questions about U.S. immigration enforcement and how it affects respondents' migration histories and future plans. While analysts must account for the likelihood that unauthorized migrants may be less than forthcoming with interviewers and may be under-represented in certain survey samples,

---

[88] For a fuller discussion, see U.S. Government Accountability Office (GAO), *Border Patrol: Key Elements of Strategic Plan not Yet in Place to Inform Border Security Status and Resource Needs*, GAO-13-25, December 2012 (hereafter: GAO, *Key Elements of Strategic Plan.*) Also see Elliot Spagat, "Under Pressure, Border Patrol Now Counts Getaways," *Associate Press*, April 22, 2013.

[89] Ibid., p. 30.

[90] Mexicans accounted for about 59% of unauthorized migrants in the United States in 2011; see Michael Hoefer, Nancy Rytina, and Bryan Baker, *Estimates of the Unauthorized Immigrant Population Residing in the United States: January 2011*, Department of Homeland Security, Office of Immigration Statistics, Washington, DC, March 2011. For a fuller discussion, see CRS Report R42560, *Mexican Migration to the United States: Policy and Trends*, by William A. Kandel, Clare Ribando Seelke, and Ruth Ellen Wasem.

[91] NRC, *Options for Estimating Illegal Entries*, pp. 5-4 – 5-15.

a body of social science research has made use of these data and developed commonly cited methodologies to account for these and other challenges.[92]

Probability of Apprehension

The UCSD and Princeton surveys both include data, based on self-reporting by people who have previously attempted to migrate illegally, on the probability that an alien will be apprehended on any given attempted crossing. According to the Princeton data, the probability of being apprehended on any given crossing averaged about .37 in the two decades before IRCA's passage, ranging from a low of .31 to a high of .42 during this period. The probability of apprehension was somewhat lower in the decade after IRCA's passage, ranging from .22 to .32 between 1986 and 1995, and averaging .26 for the decade. Between 1996 and 2010, the last year for which sufficient data are available, the apprehension rate returned to an average of .36, with a low of .29 and a high of .50 during these years.[93]

The UCSD data suggest slightly higher apprehension rates, and show broadly similar trends. According to these data, the probability of being apprehended on any given crossing averaged .51 between 1974 and 1983, ranging from .32 to .67 during this period. After peaking at .67 in 1981, the probability of apprehension fell steadily to a low of .34 in 1992-1993. Since 1994 the probability of apprehension has averaged .49, ranging from .30 to .58 during this period.[94] The UCSD and the Princeton estimates of apprehension rates are substantially lower than the Border Patrol's current estimate, which is between .67 and .86.[95]

Border Deterrence

The Princeton and UCSD surveys thus find that unauthorized migrants are apprehended about a third to one-half of the time on any given crossing attempt. Both surveys also find that most aliens who attempt to cross illegally eventually succeed, meaning border deterrence rates are low. According to the Princeton data, between 75% and 90% of aliens apprehended at the border between 1965 and 2009 made a subsequent attempt to re-enter the United States and between 55% and 88% eventually succeeded. Border deterrence (i.e., the proportion of aliens who *failed* to re-enter the United States) averaged 37% in the two decades before IRCA's passage; averaged 26% between 1986 and 1995, reaching an all-time low of 21% in 1989; and averaged 34% in 1996-2009, the last year for which sufficient data are available. The UCSD survey finds at-the-border deterrence rates below 10% for the entire post-1980 period.[96]

---

[92] See for example, Wayne A. Cornelius and Idean Salehyan, "Does border enforcement deter unauthorized immigration? The case of Mexican migration to the United States of America," *Regulation & Governance* 1.2 (2007): pp. 139-153; Manuela Angelucci, "U.S. Border Enforcement and the Net Flow of Mexican Illegal Migration," *Economic Development and Cultural Change*, 60, 2 (2012):311-357.

[93] CRS Calculations based on data provided by Princeton University Mexico Migration Project. All figures are based on three-year moving averages of annual apprehension probabilities.

[94] CRS calculations based on data provided by University of California-San Diego Mexico Migration Field Research Project. All figures are based on three-year moving averages of annual apprehension probabilities. Figures are based on total apprehensions divide by total trips, not once-or-more apprehension rates by individual migrants.

[95] Estimates provided by CBP Office of Congressional Affairs, April 24, 2013. Border Patrol reportedly estimates apprehensions using a methodology broadly similar to the capture-recapture method discussed elsewhere in this report (see **"Estimating Illegal Flows Using Recidivism Data"**).

[96] Survey data on at-the-border deterrence may under-estimate deterrence rates due to the difficulty of measuring (continued...)

Smuggling Fees

Princeton and UCSD surveys indicate that the majority of unauthorized migrants to the United States make use of human smugglers (often referred to in Mexico as "coyotes" or "polleros") to facilitate their illegal admission to the country. Indeed, whereas about 80% of unauthorized migrants from Mexico reportedly relied on human smugglers during the 1980s, about 90% did so in 2005-2007, though the use of smugglers may have declined a bit during the recent economic downturn.[97] Migrants' reliance on human smugglers, along with prices charged by smugglers, are an additional potential indicator of the effectiveness of U.S. border enforcement efforts, as more effective enforcement should increase the costs to smugglers of bringing migrants across the border, with smugglers passing such costs along to their clients in the form of higher fees.[98]

Figure 8 summarizes data from the Princeton and UCSD surveys describing average smuggling fees paid by certain unauthorized migrants from Mexico to the United States. In both cases, the data reflect reported smuggling fees based on surveys conducted with unauthorized migrants in the United States and in Mexico (i.e., after migrants had returned home), with fees adjusted for inflation and reported in 2010 dollars.

(...continued)

successful entry on a single trip, versus successful entry over the course of a lifetime.

[97] See Princeton University Mexican Migration Project, "Access to Border-Crossing Guides and Family/Friends on First Undocumented Trip," http://mmp.opr.princeton.edu/results/002coyote-en.aspx.

[98] See Bryan Roberts, Gordon Hanson, and Derekh Cornwell et al., *An Analysis of Migrant Smuggling Costs along the Southwest Border*, DHS Office of Immigration Statistics, Washington, DC, November 2010. The extent to which smugglers may pass their costs along to migrants also depends on the elasticity of migration with respect to such costs, as Roberts et al. discuss; smuggling fees may also therefore depend on the broader migration context, including economic "pulls" and "pushes" in the United States and its migration partner states.

Figure 8. Smuggling Fees Paid by Unauthorized Mexican Migrants, 1980-2010

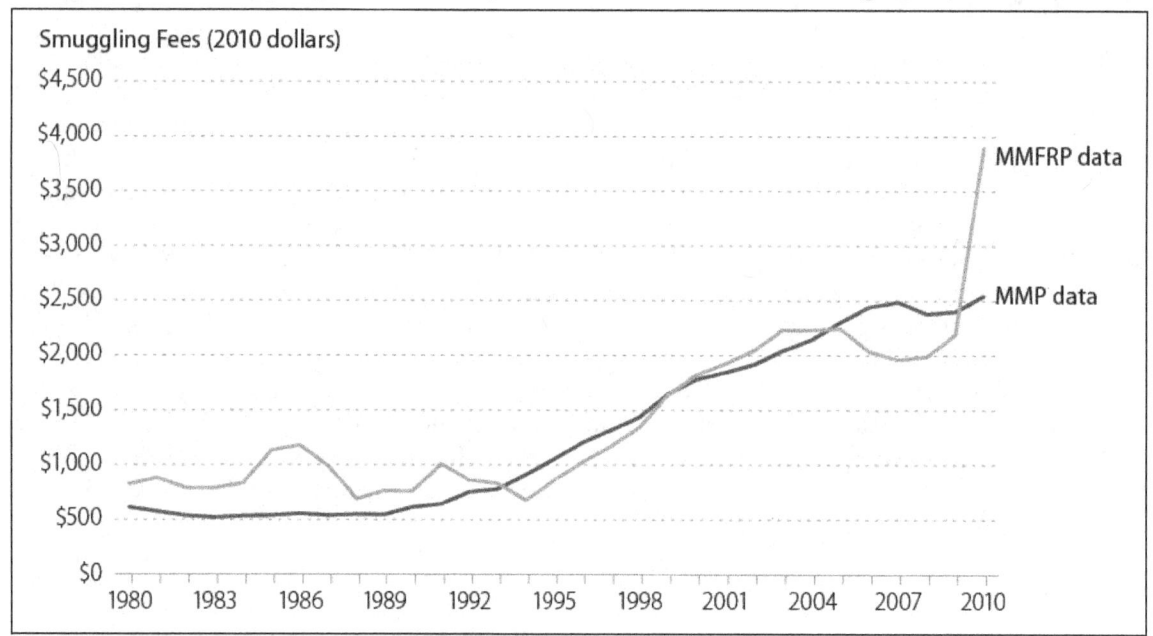

Source: Princeton University Mexican Migration Project (MMP) and University of California, San Diego Mexican Migration Field Research Program (MMFRP).

Notes: Data based on surveys of unauthorized Mexican migrants about their most recent unauthorized trip to the United States, with reported amounts adjusted for inflation using Bureau of Labor Statistics Consumer Price Index Research Series Using Current Methods (CPI-R-US). Data are a weighted three-year average to account for a small sample size. MMFRP estimate for 2010 may be unreliable due to a small sample size for that year.

According to these data, smuggling fees were mostly flat between 1980 and 1993, at about $600-$850, with an average annual real growth rate of 1.5%-02.0%. Smuggling fees in both samples began to rise beginning around 1994, and climbed by an average of 11% per year between 1994 and 2002, reaching about $2,000 in both samples by 2002. Growth in smuggling fees has been slower since then, averaging 3.7% per year in the Princeton sample and 1.8% in the UCSD sample (excluding data from 2010, a year in which a small sample may have resulted in an unreliable annual estimate).[99] Thus, these data suggest that crossing the border illegally became somewhat more difficult—or at least most expensive—in the decade after the USBP began to implement its 1994 national strategy.

Metrics of Border Security

Some Members of Congress and others have asked the Border Patrol to provide a clear measure of how many aliens cross the border illegally and/or of the overall state of border security,[100] but measuring illegal border flows is difficult for the obvious reason that unauthorized aliens seek to

---

[99] All data are CRS calculations based on data provided by Princeton University Mexico Migration Project and UCSD Mexican Migration Field Research Project.

[100] See for example, U.S. Congress, House Committee on Homeland Security, Subcommittee on Borders and Maritime Security, *Measuring Outcomes to Understand the State of Border Security*, 113th Congress, 1st sess., March 20, 2013; U.S. Congress, Senate Committee on Homeland Security and Governmental Affairs, *Border Security: Measuring Progress and Addressing the Challenges,* 113th Congress, 1st sess., March 14, 2013.

avoid detection. While the Border Patrol has accurate data on various *enforcement outcomes*, these enforcement data were not designed to measure overall *illegal inflows*. Thus, DHS officials have testified that current enforcement data do not offer a suitable metric to describe border security.[101]

Apprehensions data are imperfect indicators of illegal flows because they exclude two important groups when it comes to unauthorized migration: aliens who successfully enter and remain in the United States (i.e., enforcement failures) and aliens who are deterred from entering the United States (i.e., certain enforcement successes). Thus, analysts do not know if a decline in apprehensions is an indicator of successful enforcement, because fewer people are attempting to enter, or of enforcement failures, because more of them are succeeding.[102] A further limitation to apprehensions data is that they count events, not unique individuals, so the same person may appear multiple times in the dataset after multiple entry attempts.

Unique apprehensions and USBP's estimate of got aways and turn backs are designed, in part, to address these limitations, but they offer only partial solutions. Unique apprehensions address the "overcount" problem associated with recidivism, but still misses information about certain enforcement failures (got-aways) and certain enforcement successes (deterrence). Estimated got aways and turn backs attempt to grapple with the latter problem; but (like apprehensions) they count events rather than individuals. Moreover, because estimated got-aways and turn backs attempt to measure enforcement outcomes that do not result in apprehensions, they are heavily dependent on the subjective judgment of individual border agents.[103] To the extent that agents—or the agency—are rewarded for effective enforcement, some people may question the credibility of a measure based on such judgments. Indeed, some media reports already have raised questions about the accuracy of the got away and turn back data.[104] The Border Patrol issued new guidance in September 2012 designed to impose greater consistency on turn back and got away data collection and reporting,[105] but data from the new system have not yet been analyzed.

A further limitation of enforcement data is that all such data depend on enforcement resources. In general, USBP enforcement outcomes (e.g., apprehensions, estimated got aways) are a function of (1) the underlying illegal flows and (2) the agency's ability to detect such flows. Enforcement data alone cannot disentangle these two factors. As a result, enforcement data may tend to overestimate illegal flows where resources are robust, and to under-estimate such flows where resources are scarce.

---

[101] U.S. Congress, House Committee on Homeland Security, Subcommittee on Borders and Maritime Security, *Measuring Outcomes to Understand the State of Border Security*, testimony of Assistant Commissioner of Homeland Security Mark Borkowski, 113th Congress, 1st sess., March 20, 2013; U.S. Congress, House Committee on Homeland Security, Subcommittee on Borders and Maritime Security, *Measuring Outcomes to Understand the State of Border Security*, testimony of Border Patrol Chief Michael Fisher, 113th Congress, 1st sess., March 20, 2013. Also see U.S. Congress, House Committee on Homeland Security, Subcommittee on Border and Maritime Security, *What Does a Secure Border Look Like*, testimony by Marc R. Rosenblum, 113th Cong., 1st sess., February 26, 2013.

[102] See Edward Alden and Bryan Roberts, "Are U.S. Borders Secure? Why We Don't Know and How to Find Out," *Foreign Affairs* 90, 4 (2011): pp. 19-26.

[103] For a fuller discussion, see GAO, *Key Elements of Strategic Plan*, pp. 28-31.

[104] See for example, Andrew Becker, "New Drone Radar Reveals Border Patrol 'Gotaways' in High Numbers," *Center for Investigative Reporting*, April 4, 2013.

[105] GAO, *Key Elements of Strategic Plan*, p. 24.

Given the limits of existing border enforcement data, DHS and outside researchers have developed several different metrics for estimating illegal border flows and describing border security. Three different methods for estimating illegal migration stocks and flows are described in the remainder of this section, and broad conclusions based on these metrics are described below (see "How Secure is the U.S. Border?").[106]

The Residual Method for Estimating Unauthorized Residents in the United States

Arguably the most well-developed approach to measuring unauthorized migration focuses on the number of unauthorized migrants residing in the United States. For many years, analysts within DHS and other social scientists have used the so-called "residual method" to estimate this number. In essence, the method involves using legal admissions data to estimate the legal, foreign-born population, and then subtracting this number from the overall count of foreign-born residents based on U.S. census data.[107]

The residual method provides limited information about the border *per se* because many unauthorized residents enter the United States through ports of entry, lawfully or otherwise.[108] Nonetheless, estimates of the size of the unauthorized population may offer several advantages over the border metrics discussed below. First, for many people, how many unauthorized aliens reside within the United States ultimately is a more important question than how many cross the border. After all, if illegal border flows fall to zero, but many people continue to enter illegally through ports of entry or by overstaying nonimmigrant visas, many people would consider such an outcome problematic. Second, for this reason, the size of the unauthorized population more comprehensively reflects how well immigration policy and immigration enforcement function, including for example the effectiveness of worksite and other interior enforcement efforts as well as how well visas meet employer and family demands. Third, estimates of the unauthorized population offer the advantage of a nearly 30-year track record and a relatively uncontroversial methodology. As long ago as 2001, the Department of Justice used the total estimated stock of unauthorized migrants in the United States as a key performance metric for the department's evaluation of its border security efforts.[109]

---

[106] For a fuller discussion of border metric methodologies and additional estimates of border security, also see Bryan Roberts, John Whitley and Edward Alden, *Managing Illegal Immigration to the United States: How Effective is Enforcement?* New York: Council on Foreign Relations Press, 2013 (hereafter: Roberts et al., *Managing Illegal Immigration to the United States*).

[107] For a clear discussion of this methodology, see Jeffrey S. Passel, "The Size and Characteristics of the Unauthorized Migrant Population in the U.S.," *Pew Hispanic Center*, March 6, 2006, http://www.pewhispanic.org/2006/03/07/size-and-characteristics-of-the-unauthorized-migrant-population-in-the-us/. Also see CRS Report RL33874, *Unauthorized Aliens Residing in the United States: Estimates Since 1986*, by Ruth Ellen Wasem.

[108] In general, unauthorized migrants enter the United States three ways: by crossing the border without inspection between ports of entry (the focus of this report); by entering illegally through ports of entry, either by using a fraudulent document or by hiding in a vehicle; or by entering legally and then overstaying a temporary visa or becoming deportable for some other reason.

[109] See Department of Justice, *FY2001 Performance Report & FY2002 Revised Final, FY2003 Performance Plan*, Washington, DC 2001, pp. 120-122.

CBP Metrics of Border Security

Operational Control of the Border

Section 2 of the Secure Fence Act of 2006 (P.L. 109-367) defines operational control of the border to mean "the prevention of all unlawful entries into the United States, including entries by terrorists, other unlawful aliens, instruments of terrorism, narcotics, and other contraband." Most experts agree that preventing 100% of unlawful entries across U.S. borders is an impossible task;[110] and through FY2010, the Border Patrol classified portions of the border as being under "effective" or "operational" control if the agency "has the ability to detect, respond, and interdict illegal activity at the border or after entry into the United States."[111] The agency conducted a five-level assessment of border security, with the two top levels ("controlled" and "managed") defined as being under effective control, and the three remaining levels ("monitored," "low-level monitored," and "remote/low activity") defined as not being under effective control.[112] In February 2010, the Border Patrol reported that 1,107 miles (57%) of the Southwest border were under effective control.[113]

Beginning in FY2011, USBP stopped using this measure of effective control.[114] The agency reportedly no longer views operational or effective control as a useful metric because station and sector chiefs could not accurately and reliably use the five-level coding scheme to assess different border regions.[115] In addition, given the dynamic nature of border threats, the agency does not view it as useful to evaluate border security on a mile-by-mile basis.[116]

Border Conditions Index

In May 2011, DHS announced that CBP was developing a new "border conditions index" (BCI).[117] Reportedly, the BCI will include measures of estimated illegal flows between ports of entry, wait times and the efficiency of legal flows at ports of entry, and public safety and quality of life in border regions. These three components will be combined to develop a holistic "score" calculated for different regions of the border.[118] With these different components, the BCI

---

[110] See, for example, Edward Alden and Bryan Roberts, "Are US Borders Secure? Why We Don't Know, and How to Find Out," *Foreign Affairs*, vol. 90, no. 4 (July/August 2011), pp. 19-26.

[111] U.S. Government Accountability Office, *Border Security: Preliminary Observations on Border Control Measuers for the Southwest Border*, GAO-11-374T, February 15, 2011, p. 7.

[112] Ibid., p. 8.

[113] U.S. Congress, House Committee on Homeland Security, Subcommittee on Border and Maritime Security, *Securing Our Borders: Operational Control and the Path Forward*, 112th Congress, 1st sess., February 15, 2010.

[114] DHS did not report on border miles under effective control in its FY2010 Annual Performance Report; see DHS, *Annual Performance Report: Fiscal Years 2010-2012*, Washington, DC, April 2011, http://www.dhs.gov/xlibrary/assets/cfo_apr_fy2010.pdf.

[115] CBP Office of Congressional Affairs, March 15, 2013.

[116] U.S. Congress, House Committee on Homeland Security, Subcommittee on Borders and Maritime Security, *Measuring Outcomes to Understand the State of Border Security*, testimony of Border Patrol Chief Michael Fisher, 113th Congress, 1st sess., March 20, 2013.

[117] U.S. Congress, Senate Committee on Homeland Security and Governmental Affairs, *Securing the Border: Progress at the Federal Level*, testimony of Secretary of Homeland Security Janet Napolitano, 112th Cong., 1st sess., May 4, 2011.

[118] CBP Office of Congressional Affairs, December 9, 2011.

includes some of the same information some Members of Congress and others may consider to be of interest with respect to describing border security; but DHS officials have emphasized that the BCI encompasses a broader set of issues than "border security" as this term is normally used, and that the BCI therefore may not satisfy demands for a single comprehensive measure of border security.[119] Officials have also testified that the BCI remains in the development phase.[120]

Border Patrol Effectiveness Rate

By dividing apprehensions and estimated turn backs (i.e., successful enforcement outcomes) by estimated known illegal entries (see "Estimated "Got Aways" and "Turn Backs""), USBP calculates an *estimated enforcement effectiveness rate.* Some people have proposed using this effectiveness rate as a measure of border security. While using enforcement data to measure border security raises a number of methodological concerns (see "Metrics of Border Security"), the effectiveness *rate* would have an advantage over other enforcement metrics because, as a ratio, it may be somewhat less sensitive to the level of enforcement resources in place.[121] As with the BCI, it is difficult to evaluate USBP's effectiveness rate as a border metric because little is known about the agency's new protocols for collecting got away and turn back data.

Estimating Illegal Flows Using Recidivism Data

For many years, social scientists have used the so-called "capture-recapture" method to estimate unauthorized flows based on recidivism data.[122] The capture-recapture method estimates the total flow of unauthorized migrants based on the ratio of persons re-apprehended after an initial enforcement action to the total number of persons apprehended.[123] In the basic model, the probability of apprehension is calculated by taking the ratio of recidivist apprehensions to total apprehensions; and the total illegal inflow is calculated by dividing total apprehensions by the odds of apprehension.[124] See **Appendix** for more details.

An advantage to the capture-recapture method is that it relies on observable administrative enforcement data—apprehensions and recidivists—to calculate key border security metrics: apprehension rates and illegal flows. Yet the basic model assumes that all intending unauthorized

---

[119] U.S. Congress, House Committee on Homeland Security, Subcommittee on Borders and Maritime Security, *Measuring Outcomes to Understand the State of Border Security*, testimony of Assistant Commissioner of Homeland Security Mark Borkowski, 113th Congress, 1st sess., March 20, 2013.

[120] Ibid.

[121] That is, whereas using apprehensions as a metric of border security is problematic because apprehensions depend on border resources, the ratio of apprehensions to got aways is somewhat less problematic because both apprehensions *and* estimated known got aways depend on resources, so the ratio may more accurately reflect the proportion of aliens that successfully enters. Nonetheless, the ratio may still be sensitive to border resources if estimating inflows is less (or more) resource-intensive than apprehending aliens. And the enforcement rate by itself may not be an acceptable metric without also considering data on total illegal attempts: many would consider a 10% effectiveness rate based on 100 entry attempts to be more effective than a 90% rate based on a million attempts, for example.

[122] According to CBP Office of Congressional Affairs December 20, 2011 and more recent CRS conversations with DHS officials, DHS reportedly plans to use a capture-recapture model as one element of the border conditions index (BCI).

[123] Thomas J. Espenshade, "Using INS Border Apprehension Data to Measure the Flow of Undocumented Migrants Crossing the U.S.-Mexico Frontier," *International Migration Review*, vol. 29, no. 2 (Summer 1995), pp. 545-565.

[124] In statistical methods, the odds of apprehension equal the probability of apprehension divided by one minus the probability of apprehension; see Ibid.

---

migrants eventually succeed (i.e., that none are deterred at the border).[125] To the extent that the build-up in border enforcement resources and the deployment of the Consequence Delivery System cause some would-be unauthorized migrants to give up and return home, the capture-recapture method *underestimates* successful enforcement and *overestimates* illegal flows. Likewise, the basic model assumes that all border crossers originate in—and are repatriated to—Mexico, facilitating re-entry attempts. As the proportion of border crossers from countries other than Mexico increases—as it has in recent years—[126]repatriated aliens may be less likely to attempt re-entry, an additional reason the capture-recapture model may over-estimate illegal inflows.

Thus, to estimate illegal flows based on the capture-recapture method, enforcement data on apprehensions and repeat apprehensions must be supplemented with additional information about the proportion of migrants deterred, and must control for lower recidivism rates among non-Mexicans.[127] Estimates of illegal flows based on this methodology are discussed below (see "How Secure is the U.S. Border?").

How Secure is the U.S. Border?

While no single metric accurately and reliably describes border security (see "Metrics of Border Security"), most analysts agree, based on available data, that the number of illegal border crossers fell sharply between about 2005 and 2011, with some rise in illegal flows in 2012. This conclusion is supported by key Border Patrol enforcement data described above, including the drop in total apprehensions, the drop in unique apprehensions, and the drop in estimated got aways and total estimated known entries across eight out of nine Border Patrol sectors.

Survey data confirm an apparent drop in illegal inflows, and measure such effects away from the border. For example, according to data collected by the Princeton Mexican Migration Project, an average of about 2% of all Mexican men initiated a first unauthorized trip to the United States each year between 1973 and 2002; but that percentage has fallen sharply since 2002, to below 0.4% in 2008-2011.[128] Estimates of the unauthorized population based on the residual method report drops of about 1 million unauthorized migrants living in the United States, from about 12.4 million in 2007 to 11.1 million in 2011.[129] And the Pew Hispanic Center estimates that net (i.e.,

---

[125] Ibid. The basic model also assumes that that the odds of being apprehended are the same across different border regions and across multiple attempts to cross the border.

[126] Mexicans accounted for 87% of USBP apprehensions in FY2010, 84% in FY2011, and 73% in FY2012, the three lowest proportions ever recorded.

[127] See Roberts et al., *Managing Illegal Immigration to the United States*); Panel on Survey Options for Estimating the Flow of Unauthorized Crossings at the U.S.-Mexico Border, *Options for Estimating Illegal Entries at the U.S.-Mexico Border*, Washington, DC: National Research Council, 2012 (hereafter: NRC, *Options for Estimating Illegal Entries*). Accounting for deterrence, flows are estimated to be equal to the number of total apprehensions divided by the the odds of successful enforcement; and the probability of successful enforcement is defined as the number of recidivists divided by total apprehensions, divided by one minus the probability of deterrence.

[128] Princeton University Mexican Migration Project, "Probability of a Mexican Taking a First U.S. Trip," http://mmp.opr.princeton.edu/results/009firsttrip-en.aspx.

[129] Jeffrey Passel and D'Vera Cohn, "Unauthorized Immigrants: 11.1 Million in 2011," Pew Hispanic Center, December 6, 2012, http://www.pewhispanic.org/2012/12/06/unauthorized-immigrants-11-1-million-in-2011/; also see CRS Report RL33874, *Unauthorized Aliens Residing in the United States: Estimates Since 1986*, by Ruth Ellen Wasem.

northbound minus southbound) unauthorized migration from Mexico fell to about zero in 2011, and that outflows may have even exceeded inflows.[130]

According to GAO's analysis of Border Patrol metrics, eight out of nine Border Patrol sectors (all except the Big Bend sector) showed improved effectiveness rates between FY2006 and FY2011.[131] In the Tucson sector, the main focus of GAO's analysis, the effectiveness rate improved from 67% to 87% during this period. The San Diego, El Centro, Yuma, and El Paso sectors all had effectiveness rates in FY2011 of about 90%; the Del Rio and Laredo sectors (along with Tucson) had rates above 80%; and the Big Bend and Rio Grande Valley sectors had rates between 60% and 70%.

CRS estimates based on USBP recidivism data and using the capture-recapture method also suggest that illegal flows between ports of entry fell substantially between 2005 and 2011, before rising somewhat in 2012 (see **Figure 9**). The shaded area in **Figure 9** depicts total estimated illegal inflows, which are equal to the total number of apprehensions divided by the estimated odds of successful enforcement. (See **Appendix** for a discussion of the methodology used to generate **Figure 9**.) Based on available data, the figure assumes deterrence rates in 2000-2012 were between 20% (the estimates depicted by the upper bound of the shaded area) and 40% (the lower bound). As the figure indicates, total estimated illegal inflows fell from a high of between 760,000 and 1.4 million in 2004 to a low of between 340,000 and 580,000 in 2009-2010.[132] The model estimates that total illegal inflows were between 400,000 and 660,000 in 2012. Although recidivism data are not available to make similar calculations for previous years, apprehension levels and survey data from the 1980s and 1990s suggest that total illegal inflows likely were lower in 2007-2012 than at any other point in the last three decades.

---

[130] Jeffrey Passel, D'Vera Cohn and Ana Gonzalez-Barrera, "Net Migration from Mexico Falls to Zero—and Perhaps Less," Washington, DC: Pew Hispanic Center, May 3, 2012.

[131] GAO, *Key Elements of Strategic Plan*, pp. 74-82. Effectiveness rates in this paragraph are defined as the proportion of known illegal entrants who are apprehended or return to Mexico; effectiveness rates are lower if turn-backs are not counted in the numerator.

[132] As **Figure 9** illustrates, the model estimates that illegal inflows reached their lowest point in 2009 if deterrence is assumed to be 40%, while inflows reached their lowest point in 2011 if deterrence is assumed to be 20%.

Figure 9. Total Estimated Illegal Border Inflows, by Assumed Rate of Deterrence

FY2000-FY2012

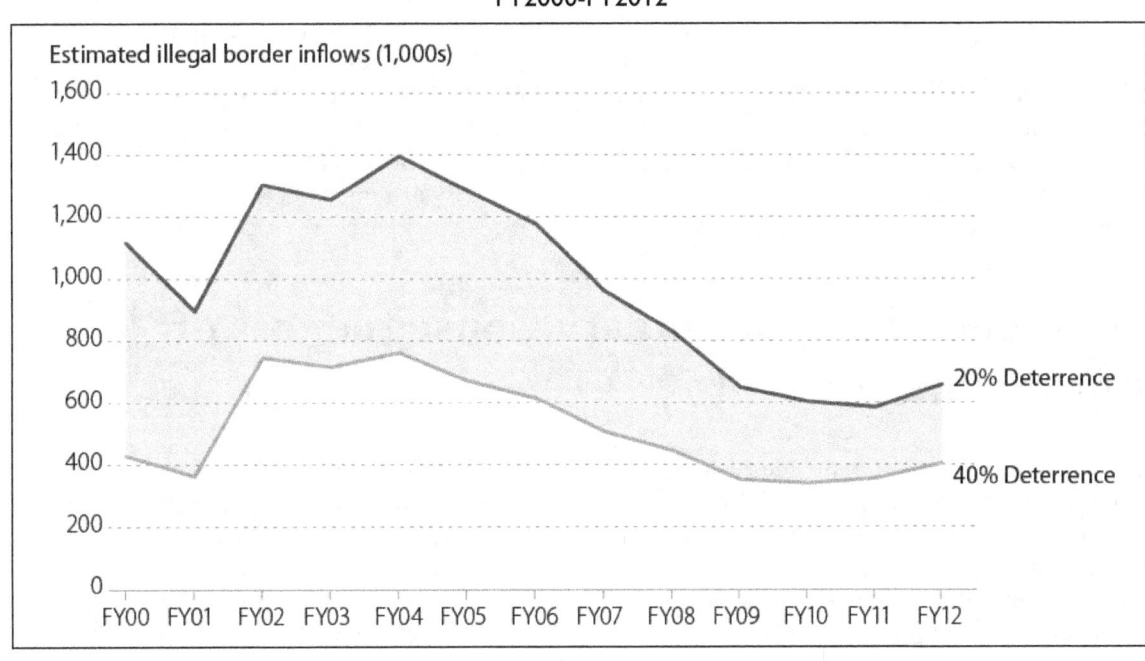

Source: CRS Analysis based on data provided by CBP Office of Congressional Affairs.

Notes: See text for discussion of methodology.

Border enforcement is only one of several factors that affect illegal migration.[133] Thus, if illegal entries indeed fell after 2006, to what degree is this change attributable to enforcement versus other developments, such as the U.S. economic downturn since 2007, and/or economic and demographic changes in Mexico and other countries of origin?[134] Disentangling the effects of enforcement from other factors influencing migration flows is particularly difficult in the current case because many of the most significant new enforcement efforts—including a sizeable share of new border enforcement personnel, most border fencing, new enforcement practices at the border, and many of the new migration enforcement measures within the United States—all have occurred at the same time as the most severe recession since the 1930s.

Nonetheless, the drop in recidivism rates suggests that an increasing proportion of aliens are being deterred by CBP's enforcement efforts, a finding that also appears to be reflected in survey data from the Princeton survey (see "Border Deterrence"). Surveys of unauthorized migrants repatriated to Mexico in 2005 and 2010 also suggest that enforcement is increasingly likely to deter future immigration.[135] As **Figure 9** illustrates, the more unauthorized migrants that are being deterred by U.S. enforcement efforts, the lower the number of successful illegal inflows.

---

[133] See, for example, Douglas S. Massey, Joaquin Arango, and Graeme Hugo et al., *Worlds In Motion: Understanding International Migration at the End of the Millenium*, 2nd ed. (New York: Oxford University Press, 2005).

[134] On the effects of Mexico's falling birthrate on U.S. immigration, see Gordon H. Hanson, Esther Duflo, and Craig McIntosh, "The Demography of Mexican Migration to the United States," *American Economic Review*, vol. 99, no. 2 (May 2009), pp. 22-27. Also see CRS Report R42560, *Mexican Migration to the United States: Policy and Trends*, by William A. Kandel, Clare Ribando Seelke, and Ruth Ellen Wasem.

[135] Among Mexicans who migrated illegally to look for work (83% of those in the survey), 60% of those repatriated in 2010 reported that they intended to return to the United States immediately, and 80% reported that they intended to (continued...)

Academic research from 2012 also provides evidence that border enforcement has contributed to a reduction in illegal flows.[136] These findings are noteworthy, in part, because they contradict earlier academic research, much of which found that border enforcement had a limited impact or even was counter-productive when it came to migration control efforts (also see "Migration Flows: "Caging" Effects and Alternative Modes of Entry").[137] This research suggests that the recent build-up in immigration enforcement at the border and within the United States may have had a greater deterrent effect on illegal migration than earlier efforts.[138] Nonetheless, some uncertainty will remain about the true level of border security as long as U.S. employment demand remains below historic levels.

Unintended and Secondary Consequences of Border Enforcement

The preceding discussion includes estimates of what may be described as the primary costs and benefits of border enforcement, defined in terms of congressional appropriations and deployment of enforcement resources on one hand, and alien apprehensions and other indicators of successful enforcement on the other. A comprehensive analysis of the costs and benefits of border enforcement policies may also consider possible unintended and secondary consequences. Such consequences may produce both costs and benefits—many of which are difficult to measure—in at least five areas: border-area crime and migrant deaths, migrant flows, environmental impacts, effects on border communities, and U.S. foreign relations.

Border-Area Crime and Migrant Deaths

Illegal border crossing is associated with a certain level of border crime and violence and, in the most unfortunate cases, with deaths of illegal border crossers and border-area law enforcement officers. Unauthorized migration may be associated with crime and mortality in several distinct ways. First, unauthorized migration is associated with crime—apart from the crime of illegal entry—because some unauthorized migrants contract with immigrant smugglers and because

---

(...continued)

return eventually, down from 81% and 92%, respectively, in 2005. Among new unauthorized migrants (those who had spent less than a week in the United States before being repatriated to Mexico), 18% of those repatriated in 2010 reported that they would *not* return to the United States compared to 6% in 2005. See Jeffrey Passel, D'Vera Cohn, and Ana Gonzalez-Barrera, *Net Migration from Mexico Falls to Zero—And Perhaps Less*, Pew Hispanic Center, Washington, DC, 2012, http://www.pewhispanic.org/files/2012/04/PHC-04-23a-Mexican-Migration.pdf, pp. 24-25.

[136] See for example, Scott Borger, Gordon Hanson, and Bryan Roberts "The Decision to Emigrate From Mexico," presentation at the Society of Government Economists annual conference, November 6, 2012; Manuela Angelucci, "U.S. Border Enforcement and the Net Flow of Mexican Illegal Migration," *Economic Development and Cultural Change*, 60, 2 (2012):311-357; Rebecca Lessem. "Mexico-US Immigration: Effects of Wages and Border Enforcement," Carnegie Mellon University, Research Showcase, May 2, 2012.

[137] See for example, Wayne Cornelius, "Evaluating Recent US Immigration Control Policy: What Mexican Migrants Can Tell Us," in *Crossing and Controlling Borders: Immigration Policies and Their Impact on Migrants' Journeys*, ed. Mechthild Baumann, Astrid Lorenz, and Kerstin Rosenhow (Farmington, MI: Budrich Unipress Ltd, 2011); Douglas S. Massey, Jorge Durand, and Nolan J. Malone, *Beyond Smoke and Mirrors: Mexican Immigration in an Era of Economic Integration* (Russell Sage Foundation, 2002).

[138] See Manuela Angelucci, "U.S. Border Enforcement and the Net Flow of Mexican Illegal Migration," *Economic Development and Cultural Change*, 60, 2 (2012):311-357.

---

unauthorized migrants may engage in related illegal activity, such as document fraud. Yet fear of the police may make unauthorized aliens *less* likely to engage in other types of criminal activity, and research on the subject finds low immigrant criminality rates, especially when accounting for education levels and other demographic characteristics.[139] Second, illegal border crossers face risks associated with crossing the border at dangerous locations, where they may die from exposure or from drowning.[140]

Border *enforcement* therefore may affect crime and migrant mortality in complex ways.[141] On one hand, the concentration of enforcement resources around the border may exacerbate adverse outcomes by making migrants more likely to rely on smugglers, as noted above (see "Smuggling Fees"). The 1994 National Strategic Plan *predicted* a short-term rise in border violence for these reasons.[142] On the other hand, to the extent that enforcement successfully deters illegal crossers, such prevention should reduce crime and mortality. The concentration of law enforcement personnel near the border may further enhance public safety and migrant protection, especially where CBP has made a priority of protecting vulnerable populations.[143]

The empirical record suggests that there is *no significant difference* in the average violent crime rate in border and non-border metropolitan areas.[144] Indeed, the border cities El Paso, TX, and San Diego, CA, are regularly listed among the safest large cities in the country based on their rankings among similarly sized cities in the Federal Bureau of Investigation's Uniform Crime Report.[145] The specific impact of border enforcement on border-area crime is unknown, however, because available data cannot separate the influence of border enforcement from other factors.[146]

---

[139] See CRS Report R42057, *Interior Immigration Enforcement: Programs Targeting Criminal Aliens*, by William A. Kandel.

[140] In 2011, for example, of the 238 migrants deaths for which DHS was able to determine a cause of death, 139 were attributed to exposure to heat or cold or water-related; data provided to CRS by CBP Office of Congressional Affairs December 15, 2011.

[141] Also see Karl Eschbach, Jacqueline Hagan, and Nestor Rodriguez et al., "Death at the Border," *International Migration Review*, vol. 33, no. 2 (Summer 1999), pp. 430-454.

[142] National Strategic Plan, p. 11-12.

[143] The USBP's Border Patrol Search, Trauma, and Rescue Unit (BORSTAR) is comprised of agents with specialized skills and training for tactical medical search and rescue operations. BORSTAR agents provide rapid response to search and rescue and medical operations, including rescuing migrants in distress.

[144] For a fuller discussion, see CRS Report R41075, *Southwest Border Violence: Issues in Identifying and Measuring Spillover Violence*, by Kristin Finklea.

[145] See for example, Daniel Borunda, "El Paso Ranked Safest Large city in U.S. for 3rd Straight Year," *El Paso Times*, February 6, 2013, http://www.elpasotimes.com/ci_22523903/el-paso-ranked-safest-large-city-u-s.

[146] Uniform Crime Report (UCR) data provide the most information about crime rates, but they are not sufficiently fine-tuned to provide information on the diverse factors affecting such trends; see CRS Report RL34309, *How Crime in the United States Is Measured*, by Nathan James and Logan Rishard Council.

Figure 10. Known Migrant Deaths, Southwest Border, 1985-2012

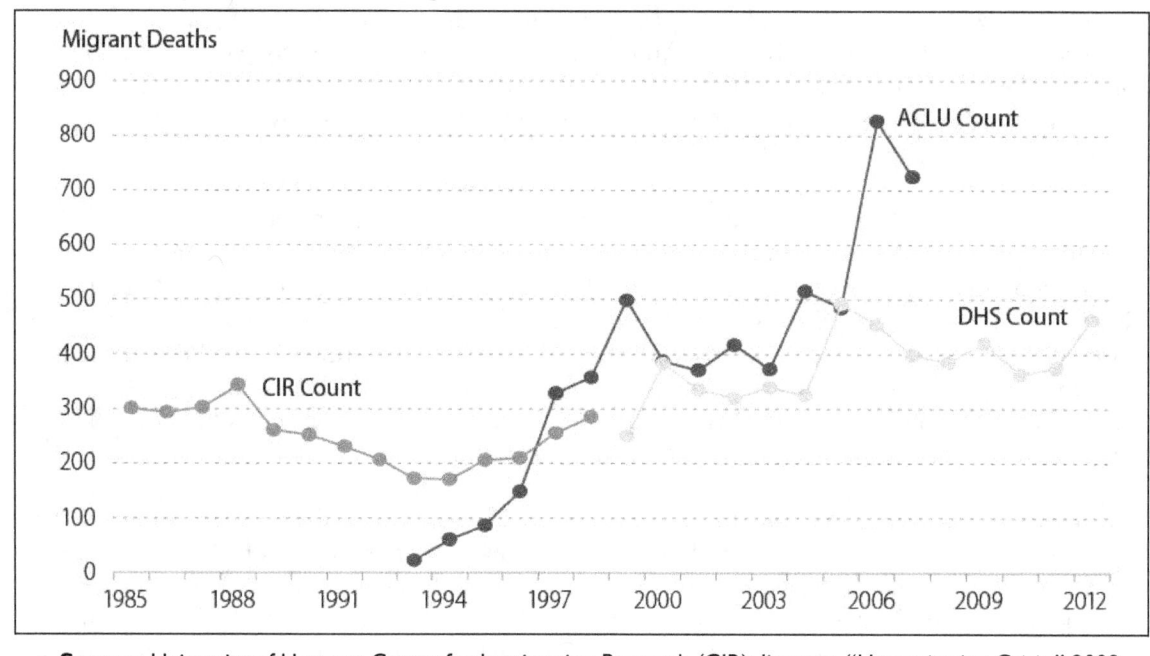

Source: University of Houston Center for Immigration Research (CIR); Jimenez, "Humanitarian Crisis," 2009 (ACLU); CBP Office of Congressional Affairs March 13, 2013 (DHS).

With respect to mortality, available data about migrant deaths along the Southwest border are presented in **Figure 10**. The figures come from academic research based on local medical investigators' and examiners' offices in California, Arizona, New Mexico, and Texas between 1985 and 1998 (the University of Houston's Center for Immigration Research, CIR); Mexican foreign ministry and Mexican media counts compiled by the American Civil Liberties Union of San Diego; and data compiled by DHS based on bodies recovered on the U.S. side of the border.[147] All three data sources reflect *known* migrant deaths, and therefore undercount actual migrant deaths since some bodies may not be discovered.[148] Additionally, U.S. data sources generally do not include information from the Mexican side of the border and therefore further undercount migration-related fatalities.

As **Figure 10** illustrates, data from the CIR indicate that known migrant deaths fell from a high of 344 in 1988 to a low of 171 in 1994 before climbing back to 286 in 1998. According to DHS data, known migrant deaths climbed from 250 in 1999 to 492 in 2005, and averaged 431 deaths per year in 2005-2009. DHS's count fell to an average of 369 per year in 2010-2011, but increased to 463 in FY2012. And the ACLU found that known migrant deaths increased from just 80 per year in 1993-1996 to 496 per year in 1997-2007. The apparent increase in migrant deaths is noteworthy in light of the apparent decline in unauthorized entries during the same period. These

---

[147] See Stanley Bailey, Karl Eschbach, and Jacqueline Hagan et al., "Migrant Death on the US-Mexco Border 1985-1996," *University of Houston Center for Immigration Research Working Paper Series*, vol. 96, no. 1 (1996); Jimenez, "Humanitarian Crisis," 2009.

[148] The Border Patrol has drawn criticism from human rights activists who claim that the agency's migrant death count understates the number of fatalities. Some contend that the Border Patrol undercounts fatalities by excluding skeletal remains, victims in car accidents, and corpses discovered by other agencies or local law enforcement officers; see , for example, Raymond Michalowski, "Border Militarization and Migrant Suffering: A Case of Transnational Social Injury," *Social Justice*, Summer 2007.

data offer evidence that border crossings have become more hazardous since the "prevention through deterrence" policy went into effect in the 1990s,[149] though (as with crime) the precise impact of enforcement on migrant deaths is unknown.

Migration Flows: "Caging" Effects and Alternative Modes of Entry

With illegal border crossing becoming more dangerous and more expensive, some unauthorized aliens appear to have adapted their behavior to avoid crossing the border via traditional pathways. Most notably, social science research suggests that border enforcement has had the unintended consequence of encouraging unauthorized aliens to settle permanently in the United States rather than working temporarily and then returning home, as was more common prior to the mid-1980s.[150] The primary evidence for this so-called "caging" effect is that unauthorized migrants appear to be staying longer in the United States and raising families here more often rather than making regular trips to visit families that remain in countries of origin.[151] Although other factors also likely contribute to these changes,[152] survey results appear to confirm that border enforcement has been a factor behind these longer stays.[153]

A second unintended consequence of enhanced border enforcement between ports of entry may have been an increase in illegal entries through ports of entry and other means. According to UCSD Mexico Migration Field Research Program research, unauthorized Mexican migrants from one community in Mexico interviewed in 2009 used six different methods to enter the United States illegally, with one in four such aliens passing illegally through a port of entry by using borrowed or fraudulent documents or by hiding in a vehicle.[154] Based on three different surveys conducted between 2008 and 2010, UCSD researchers found that the probability of being

---

[149] Also see Adam Isacson and Maureen Meyer, "Border Security and Migration: A Report from South Texas," *Washington Office on Latin America*, http://www.wola.org/sites/default/files/downloadable/Mexico/2013/Border%20Security%20and%20Migration%20South%20Texas.pdf.

[150] See Wayne Cornelius, "Evaluating Recent US Immigration Control Policy: What Mexican Migrants Can Tell Us," in *Crossing and Controlling Borders: Immigration Policies and Their Impact on Migrants' Journeys*, ed. Mechthild Baumann, Astrid Lorenz, and Kerstin Rosenhow (Farmington, MI: Budrich Unipress Ltd, 2011); Douglas S. Massey, Jorge Durand, and Nolan J. Malone, *Beyond Smoke and Mirrors: Mexican Immigration in an Era of Economic Integration* (Russell Sage Foundation, 2002).

[151] Whereas almost half of unauthorized aliens from Mexico who arrived in 1980 remained in the United States for less than a year, fewer than 20% of unauthorized Mexicans who entered in 2010 returned home within a year; see Mexican Migration Project, "Probability of Return within 12 Months," http://mmp.opr.princeton.edu/results/010returnpers-en.aspx. Also see Jonathan Hicken, Mollie Cohen, and Jorge Narvaez, "Double Jeopardy: How U.S. Enforcement Policies Shape Tunkaseño Migration," in *Mexican Migration and the U.S. Economic Crisis*, ed. Wayne A. Cornelius, David FitzGerald, Pedro Lewin Fischer, and Leah Muse-Orlinoff (La Jolla, CA: University of California, San Diego Center for Comparative Immigration Studies, 2010), pp. 56-57. And whereas an estimated 60-90% of unauthorized migrants during the 1970s were single men, by 2008 men only accounted for an estimated 53% of unauthorized aliens, with women representing 34% and the remainder children; see Jeffrey S. Passel and D'Vera Cohn, *A Portrait of Unauthorized Immigrants in the United States*, Pew Hispanic Center, Washington, DC, April 14, 2009, p. 4, http://pewhispanic.org/files/reports/107.pdf.

[152] For example, changes in U.S. labor markets have resulted in more permanent (non-seasonal) employment opportunities for unauthorized aliens as well as more employment opportunities for unauthorized women; See CRS Report R41592, *The U.S. Foreign-Born Population: Trends and Selected Characteristics*, by William A. Kandel.

[153] Half of the Mexico-based family members of unauthorized aliens interviewed by the UC, San Diego MMFRP in 2009 indicated that they had a relative who had remained in the United States longer than they had intended because they feared they would be unable to reenter the United States if they returned home; see Hicken et al. "Double Jeopardy," 57-58.

[154] Hicken et al., "Double Jeopardy," pp. 60-61.

---

apprehended while passing illegally though a port of entry was about half as high as the probability of being apprehended while crossing between the ports.[155] CBP's Passenger Compliance Examination (COMPEX) System reportedly detects very little illegal migration through ports of entry, however.[156] There is also anecdotal evidence that unauthorized aliens have recently turned to maritime routes as alternative strategies to cross the U.S.-Mexican border.[157]

Environmental Impact

A third set of potential unintended consequences concern the effect of border enforcement on the environment. As with the effects of enforcement on border crime and violence, the effects of enforcement on the environment are complex because they reflect changes in migrant behavior and the secondary effects of enforcement per se.

On one hand, many illegal border crossers transit through sensitive environmental areas, cutting vegetation for shelter and fire, potentially causing wildfires, increasing erosion through repeated use of trails, and discarding trash.[158] Thus, to the extent that border enforcement successfully deters illegal flows, enforcement benefits the environment by reducing these undesirable outcomes. On the other hand, the construction of fencing, roads, and other tactical infrastructure may damage border-area ecosystems. These environmental considerations may be especially important because much of the border runs through remote and environmentally sensitive areas.[159] For this reason, even when accounting for the possible environmental benefits of reduced illegal border flows, some environmental groups have opposed border infrastructure projects because they threaten rare and endangered species as well as other wildlife by damaging ecosystems and restricting the movement of animals, and because surveillance towers and artificial night lighting have detrimental effects on migrant birds.[160]

Effects on Border Communities and Civil Rights

Although economists disagree about the overall economic impact of unauthorized migration, unauthorized migrants may impose a number of costs at the local level, including through their use of schools and other public programs.[161] Some are also concerned that illegal migration

---

[155] Probability of apprehension on an alien's most recent attempt to illegally pass through a port of entry was 0.36, compared to 0.73 on the most recent entry attempt between ports of entry; UC San Diego MMFRP data provided to CRS September 23, 2010.

[156] CBP Office of Congressional Affairs March 21, 2013.

[157] See for example, Adolfo Flores and Ruben Vives, "New Panga Incident Investigated as Possible Smuggling Operation," *Los Angeles Times*, December 10, 2012; Dave Graham, "By Land or by Sea, Tougher U.S. Border Tests Illegal Immigrants," *Reuters*, March 20, 2013. Border tunnels are mainly used to smuggle narcotics into the United States, rather than for illegal migration.

[158] Department of Homeland Security, *Environmental Impact Statement for the Completion of the 14-mile Border Infrastructure System, San Diego, California* (July 2003), pp. 1-11.

[159] According to the GAO, about 25% of the northern border and 43% of the Southwest border consist of federal and tribal lands overseen by the U.S. Forest Service and Department of the Interior; see CRS Report R42346, *Federal Land Ownership: Overview and Data*, by Carol Hardy Vincent and Laura A. Hanson.

[160] See for example, University of Texas School of Law, "The Texas-Mexico Border Wall," http://www.utexas.edu/law/centers/humanrights/borderwall/.

[161] See CRS Report R42053, *Fiscal Impacts of the Foreign-Born Population*, by William A. Kandel. Although the overall economic effects of migration—and unauthorized migration in particular—are difficult to estimate, research suggests that fiscal costs of migration are disproportionately borne at the local level.

undermines the rule of law. For these reasons, successful border enforcement may benefit border communities by reducing illegal inflows.

Yet some business owners on the Southwest and Northern borders have complained that certain border enforcement efforts threaten their economic activities, including farming and ranching activities that are disrupted by the deployment of USBP resources to the border and commercial activities that suffer from reduced regional economic activity.[162] More generally, some people have complained that the construction of barriers divides communities that have straddled international land borders for generations.[163]

Some people have raised additional concerns about the effects of border enforcement on civil rights. Some residents of Southwest and Northern border communities see enhanced border enforcement as leading to racial profiling and wrongful detentions.[164] On top of this general concern, some people argue that Operation Streamline raises additional questions about whether migrants receive adequate legal protections during fast-tracked criminal procedures.[165] And some have argued that mistreatment and abuse are widespread in CBP detention facilities.[166]

An additional concern that some have raised about CBP's focus on high consequence enforcement is the possibility that focusing scarce judicial and prosecutorial resources on immigration enforcement diverts attention from more serious crimes.[167] A 2013 Justice Department study found that the number of immigration defendants in federal courts increased 664% between 1995 and 2010 (from 5,103 to 39,001); and that immigration cases accounted for 60% of the overall increase in pretrial detentions during that period.[168] More generally, immigration offenders accounted for 46% of federal arrests in 2010, outnumbering all other crimes and up from 22% a decade earlier.[169] A 2008 study by the Administrative Office of the U.S. Courts found that while Congress had provided short-term funding to allow the courts to

---

[162] See, for example, Mark Harrison, "Beefed Up Border Patrol Jolts Farmers, Cows," *Seattle Times*, November 13, 2011; Rafael Carranza, "Leaders Blame Lost Business Deals on Border Fence," *KGBT Channel 4 News*, November 2, 2009, http://www.valleycentral.com/news/story.aspx?id=371266#.Tt0oAmNM8rs.

[163] See, for example, Associated Press, "Quebec-Vermont Border Communities Divided by Post-9/11 Security," *CBC News: Canada*, August 14, 2011.

[164] See, for example, NY School of Law, NY Civil Liberties Union, and Families for Freedom, *Justice Derailed: What Raids On New York's Trains And Buses Reveal About Border Patrol's Interior Enforcement Practices*, New York: November, 2011, http://www.nyclu.org/publications/report-justice-derailed-what-raids-trains-and-buses-reveal-about-border-patrols-interi; Lornet Turnbull and Roberto Daza, "Climate of Fear Grips Forks Illegal Immigrants," *Seattle Times*, June 26, 2011.

[165] See for example, American Civil Liberties Union, "Immigration Reform Should Eliminate Operation Streamline," http://www.aclu.org/files/assets/operation_streamline_issue_brief.pdf.

[166] See for example, Alan Gomez, "Lawsuits Allege abuses by Border Patrol Agents," *USA Today*, March 13, 2013; Judith Greene and Alexis Mazón, "Privately Operated Federal Prisons for Immigrants: Expensive, Unsafe, Unenecessary," *Justice Strategies,* September 13, 2012; No More Deaths/No Mas Muertes, *A Culture of Cruelty: Abuse and Impunity in Short-Term U.S. Border Patrol Custody*, 2011.

[167] See, for example, National Immigration Forum, *Operation Streamline: Unproven Benefits Outweighed by Costs to Taxpayers*, Washington, DC, September 2012.

[168] Thomas H. Cohen, *Special Report: Pretrial Detention and Misconduct in Federal District Courts, 1995-2010*, U.S. Department of Justice, Bureau of Justice Statistics, NCJ 239673, Washington, DC, February 2013.

[169] Mark Motivans, *Immigration Offenders in the Federal Justice System, 2010*, U.S. Department of Justice, Bureau of Justice Statistics, NCJ 238581, Washington, DC, July 2012.

---

respond to increased prosecutions, the courts faced a shortage of suitable courthouse and detention facilities in some border locations.[170]

Effects on Regional Relations

What are the effects of U.S. border enforcement policies on U.S. relations with its continental neighbors, Mexico and Canada? The United States and Canada have a strong record of collaborative border enforcement, including through 15 binational, multi-agency Integrated Border Enforcement Teams (IBETs) operating at 24 locations at and between U.S.-Canadian ports of entry. In February 2011, President Obama and Prime Minister Harper signed the Beyond the Border declaration, which described their shared visions for a common approach to perimeter security and economic competitiveness; and the countries released an Action Plan on December 7, 2011, to implement the agreement.[171] While some Canadians have raised objections to some of the information sharing and joint law enforcement provisions of the agreement,[172] border enforcement between the ports has not been identified as a significant source of bilateral tension.

The United States and Mexico also cooperate extensively on border enforcement operations at the Southwest border.[173] Yet immigration enforcement occasionally has been a source of bilateral tension. And with Mexicans being the most frequent target of U.S. immigration enforcement efforts, some Mexicans have expressed concerns about the construction of border fencing, the effects of border enforcement on migrant deaths, and the protection of unaccompanied minors and other vulnerable groups, among other issues related to immigration enforcement.[174]

Conclusion: Understanding the Costs and Benefits of Border Enforcement between Ports of Entry

The United States has focused substantial resources along its land borders to prevent and control illegal migration since the 1980s, with investments in personnel, fencing, and surveillance assets all up significantly in the post 9/11 period, in particular. Since 2005, CBP also has transformed its approach to managing enforcement outcomes, through its Consequence Delivery System.

Measuring the *effects* of border enforcement is difficult. On one hand, after reaching a high point in 2000, Border Patrol apprehensions fell sharply in 2007-2011, reaching a 42-year low in FY2011. The Border Patrol's IDENT database also indicates a declining proportion of aliens is

---

[170] Administrative Office of the U.S. Courts, *Report on the Impact on the Judiciary of Law Enforcement Activities Along the Southwest Border*, Washington, DC: Administrative Office of the U.S. Courts, July 2008.

[171] DHS, "Beyond the Border Action Plan," December 2011, http://www.dhs.gov/files/publications/beyond-the-border-action-plan.shtm; also see CRS Report 96-397, *Canada-U.S. Relations*, coordinated by Carl Ek and Ian F. Fergusson.

[172] See for example, Dana Gabriel, "Toward a North American Police State and Security Perimeter: U.S.-Canada 'Beyond the Border Agreement,'" *Global Research*, May 14, 2012.

[173] See CRS Report R41349, *U.S.-Mexican Security Cooperation: The Mérida Initiative and Beyond*, by Clare Ribando Seelke and Kristin Finklea.

[174] See CRS Report R42560, *Mexican Migration to the United States: Policy and Trends*, by William A. Kandel, Clare Ribando Seelke, and Ruth Ellen Wasem; Marc R. Rosenblum, *Obstacles and Opportunities for Regional Cooperation: The US-Mexico Case*, Migration Policy Institute, April 2011, http://www.migrationpolicy.org/pubs/USMexico-cooperation.pdf.

---

apprehended more than once (i.e., recidivism is down). Estimates based on enforcement and survey data and accounting for estimated apprehension and deterrence rates suggest that total illegal inflows in 2009-2011 were well below levels observed in the two decades after IRCA's passage, but that illegal inflows increased somewhat in 2012.

On the other hand, there is also some evidence that migrants have adapted to more difficult conditions at the border by using other means to enter the United States and by remaining longer. A comprehensive accounting also may consider various potential unintended consequences of border enforcement on the civil rights of legal residents and U.S. citizens in the border region, on migrants' human rights, on the quality of life in border communities, on the environment and wildlife, and on U.S.-regional relations.

What do these findings mean for Members of Congress who oversee border security and immigration policy? Especially in light of current fiscal constraints, some Members of Congress may evaluate future border enforcement in terms of expected returns on America's investments, and they may consider the possibility that certain additional investments at the border may be met with diminishing returns. Border infrastructure may offer an example: with 651 miles of fencing and barriers already in place along the Southwest border, each additional mile would be in ever more remote locations, and therefore more expensive to install and maintain and likely to deter fewer unauthorized migrants. Similarly, some Members of Congress may question the concrete benefits of deploying more sophisticated surveillance systems across the entire northern and southern borders, including vast regions in which too few personnel are deployed to respond to the occasional illegal entry that may be detected.

Deciding how to allocate border resources therefore requires a clear definition of the goals of border security. Zero admissions of unauthorized migrants may not be a realistic goal when it comes to migration control, as noted above, and is a higher standard than is expected of most law enforcement agencies. While this report focuses on migration control at U.S. borders, border security also encompasses the detection and interdiction of weapons of mass destruction (WMD), narcotics, and other illicit goods; policies to combat human trafficking; and other security goals. These diverse goals are often conflated in an undifferentiated debate about "border security"; but each of these goals may suggest a different mix of border investments, as well as different metrics and different standards for successful enforcement outcomes. Should policies to prevent unauthorized migration be held to the same standards as policies to prevent the entry of WMDs, for example?

Regardless of how these questions are answered in principle, debates about immigration control and border security may benefit from better metrics of border security and illegal migration, and from a more analytical approach to program design. The Border Patrol has taken a step in this direction by analyzing recidivism data as a function of different enforcement outcomes through its Consequence Delivery System. This report also identifies several metrics for measuring border security, all of which have advantages and disadvantages. In the context of immigration policy and a possible immigration reform bill, Members of Congress may choose to focus on the total number of unauthorized aliens in the United States, in addition to border flows, since border enforcement is just one of many factors (along with interior enforcement, visa policies, etc.) influencing the size of the unauthorized population, and because more is known about the population number than about border flows.

Appendix. Capture-Recapture Methodology

The capture-recapture methodology for estimating unauthorized migration flows based on total and recidivist alien apprehensions was first proposed by the sociologist Thomas Espenshade in 1995.[175] Espenshade's original model assumed that all intending migrants (i.e., everyone who makes an initial crossing attempt) eventually succeed—an assumption supported by academic research at the time.[176] Likewise, the model focused exclusively on unauthorized Mexican migrants, a population of particular interest since Mexicans represented 96% of all alien apprehensions during the 1990s,[177] and since Mexico's long shared border with the United States creates unique enforcement dynamics, including high recidivism rates.

The basic capture-recapture model works backwards from the total number of apprehensions and recidivist apprehensions to calculate total illegal flow and the odds of apprehension. First, by definition, the number of apprehensions is related to the total number of illegal crossings multiplied by the probability of being apprehended on any given attempt. For example, if 1,000 aliens attempt to cross, and the probability of being apprehended on a given trip is 50%, then the number of apprehensions would be 500. If unsuccessful migrants always make a second (and subsequent) attempt to enter, the number of aliens making a second attempt is equal to number of initial apprehensions (i.e., 500 in the previous example); and the number of apprehensions among one-time repeat crossers would be 250. In the following period, 250 would attempt entry and 125 would succeed, and so on. By adding up these iterations, Espenshade shows that the total number of apprehensions (A) is equal to the total flow of unauthorized aliens (F) times the odds of apprehension, where odds are defined statistically as the probability of apprehension (P) divided by one minus the probability of apprehension.[178] Re-arranging this statement to solve for flow:

$$F = A/[P/(1-P)] \qquad (1)$$

Second, the ratio of repeat apprehensions to total apprehensions is used to calculate the probability of apprehension on a given attempt. In short, the formula for repeat apprehensions is simply the formula for total apprehensions times the probability of being apprehended. As a result, repeat apprehensions (R) divided by total apprehensions (A) yields the probability of apprehension ($P_{apprenehsion}$) on a given trip:[179]

$$P_{apprenehsion} = R/A \qquad (2)$$

The methodology used in this report adapts Espenshade's model to account for the fact that some aliens do not make a second or subsequent attempt after being apprehended—that is, that some are deterred.[180] This modified capture-recapture model also has been used in a 2013 Council on

---

[175] Thomas J. Espenshade, "Using INS Border Apprehension Data to Measure the Flow of Undocumented Migrants Crossing the U.S.-Mexico Frontier," *International Migration Review*, vol. 29, no. 2 (Summer 1995), pp. 545-565.

[176] Ibid., pp. 549-550.

[177] CRS analysis of apprehensions data from DHS, *Yearbook of Immigration Statistics FY2011*, Washington, DC: DHS, 2012. Mexicans accounted for 90% of all apprehensions in 2000-2009, before falling to 83% in 2010 and 76% in FY2011. (Mexicans represent a lower proportion of all apprehensions than of Border Patrol apprehensions; total apprehensions data for FY2012 were not available when this report was released.)

[178] Espenshade, "Using INS Border Apprehension Data," pp. 551-552.

[179] Ibid., p. 554.

[180] The Consequence Delivery System seeks to reduce recidivism by increasing the proportion of aliens subject to (continued...)

Foreign Relations report;[181] and DHS officials have indicated that DHS's Border Conditions Index, now under development, employs a similar method to estimate illegal flows between ports of entry.[182] In the modified model, the estimated probability of apprehension defined in equation (2) is divided by one minus the probability of deterrence to calculate the probability of successful enforcement ($P_{enforcement}$):

$$P_{enforcement} = (R/A)/(1-D) \qquad\qquad (3)$$

Figure 9 in this report was generated by using equation (3) to estimate the probability of successful enforcement at the Southwest border and equation (1) to estimate total Southwest border illegal flows. In the absence of country-specific recidivism rates (and in light of the higher costs to reentry following deportation of non-Mexicans), CRS's analysis assumes non-Mexicans do not re-enter in the same fiscal year. Thus, the calculations for equation (3) use CBP data on total recidivists divided by CBP data on Mexican apprehensions to calculate a Mexico-specific apprehension rate.[183] Based on available survey and USBP turn back data, deterrence rates were assumed to fall between 20 and 40%. CRS further assumed that Mexican and non-Mexican aliens are apprehended at the same rate, and thus uses the value of P calculated in equation (3), along with CBP data on total Southwest border apprehensions, to estimate total Southwest border illegal inflows based on equation (1).

(...continued)

formal removal, criminal charges, and/or remote repatriation (see "**CBP Consequence Delivery System**"). And unauthorized aliens from countries other than Mexico (i.e., 73% of USBP apprehensions in FY2012) typically are deported to their home countries, substantially raising the cost of re-entry.

[181] Roberts et al., *Managing Illegal Immigration to the United States.*

[182] CBP Office of Congressional Affairs, December 20, 2011.

[183] DHS also reportedly restricts its recidivism analysis to Mexican aliens, but may uses country-specific recidivism data to calculate apprehension rates, and may therefore estimate a somewhat lower probability of successful enforcement based on this methodology.

Author Contact Information

Lisa Seghetti
Section Research Manager
lseghetti@crs.loc.gov, 7-4669

Acknowledgments

Marc R. Rosenblum, a former CRS Specialist in Immigration Policy, was the original author of this report. Portions of this report are based on archived CRS Report RL32562, Border Security: The Role of the U.S. Border Patrol, by former CRS analyst Chad C. Haddal; and on archived CRS Report RL22659, *Border Security: Barriers Along the U.S. International Border*, by former CRS analyst Chad C. Haddal and CRS Legislative Attorney Michael Garcia.

CRS Graphics Specialist Amber Hope Wilhelm prepared the figures for this report.